The search for tolerance

The search for tolerance

Challenging and changing racist attitudes and behaviour among young people

Gerard Lemos
Lemos&Crane

JOSEPH ROWNTREE
FOUNDATION

The **Joseph Rowntree Foundation** has supported this project as part of its programme of research and innovative development projects, which it hopes will be of value to policy makers, practitioners and service users. The facts presented and views expressed in this report are, however, those of the author and not necessarily those of the Foundation.

Joseph Rowntree Foundation
The Homestead
40 Water End
York YO30 6WP
Website: www. jrf.org.uk

A CIP catalogue record for this report is available from the British Library.

ISBN 1 85935 284 7   (paperback)
ISBN 1 85935 285 5   (pdf: available at www.jrf.org.uk)

Cover design by Adkins Design

Prepared and printed by:
York Publishing Services Ltd
64 Hallfield Road
Layerthorpe
York YO31 7ZQ
Tel: 01904 430033; Fax: 01904 430868; Website: www.yps-publishing.co.uk

Further copies of this report, or any other JRF publication, can be obtained either from the JRF website (www.jrf.org.uk/bookshop/) or from our distributor, York Publishing Services Ltd, at the above address.

Contents

Acknowledgements

Paul Maginn worked with me on the early stages of the project. His drive and determination sought out suitable projects for case studies and persuaded teachers, youth workers and police officers to work with us on collecting substantial datasets particularly in Stafford and Peterborough. He also successfully negotiated access to young people in communities and it was his sensitive approach that brought from those young people complex insights about troubling matters. As the data was collected, his reflections about what we were finding out and, more importantly, what it all meant guided my thoughts and led me to some of the preliminary conclusions that have proved tenacious and convincing throughout the life of the project. His sense of inquiry, commitment, openness and good nature are all intensely admirable, and I owe him a great debt of gratitude.

Matt Gitsham completed the qualitative fieldwork in Rochdale, Tower Hamlets and the young offenders institution, again with sensitivity and skill in negotiating access and in the conduct of the fieldwork itself. He also put many long, trying, technical hours into analysing the enormous amount of quantitative and qualitative data we gathered. Much of the analysis is based on his work. Based on that analysis, the structure for the early drafts of this text was also his inception. He is a first-class researcher and, again, I owe him an enormous debt of gratitude.

A number of other researchers at Lemos&Crane helped with the project at various times and, in the latter stages, Shirley Rojas and Gayle Munro worked on the final drafts. I want to thank all of them.

The Joseph Rowntree Foundation provided the funds for the research and Alison Jarvis, now a long-standing collaborator of mine, was patient in her search for rigour and supportive in our search for knowledge and originality. I am very grateful to her for her contributions to the project, leading the project advisory group and commenting positively on numerous drafts, always with the greatest good humour. The project advisory group was also positive as well as challenging and worked hard on the report, particularly Keith Kirby and Kate Gavron. I want to thank them.

Finally my biggest debt of gratitude is owed to more than 600 young people who took part in the range of research activities we have engaged in and the teachers, youth workers and police officers who assisted us in our efforts to find out what young people think. I particularly want to thank all of them.

Introduction

Successive governments since the 1970s have had a policy goal of reducing unfair racial discrimination. The emphasis is now changing and being placed on building shared values and encouraging mutual respect – living together in cohesive communities, not just avoiding unfair treatment. Against the backdrop of an increasingly diverse society in which changed social attitudes have made some expressions of racism unacceptable to most people, positively influencing the attitudes and behaviour of young people about race and racism is thought appropriate for and susceptible to public policy. Multicultural education, in one form or another, stretches back many decades in UK schools. The most recent incarnations are citizenship education and personal, health and social education (PHSE). Criminal justice policy also concerns itself with the attitudes and behaviour of young people towards race and racism. The Crime and Disorder Act 1998 created a range of racially aggravated offences. If young people are convicted of these offences, the probation service and youth offending teams have a legitimate interest in seeking to change that behaviour with a view to reducing the likelihood of reoffending. With this objective in mind, a growing body of work is being delivered principally by probation officers. Community cohesion is the third relevant policy strand. Following the disorders in 2001, a range of government initiatives have been launched under this rubric. These are designed to reduce tensions and divisions in communities. Eventually, beyond a reduction in tension and disorder, the hope is that community cohesion initiatives can build a sense of common citizenship, which includes responsibilities as well as rights, based on values that are shared across religious, cultural and other differences.

This research looks at the experience of young people in programmes in all three policy streams: educational initiatives, programmes designed to change the racist behaviour of young offenders and activities that sought to build community cohesion.

Background and objectives of the research

Some current approaches contain an implicit notion of a race problem: children and young people express racially motivated prejudices or hostility and therefore are believed to have the 'wrong' idea about racial diversity and racism. Adults in authority therefore feel the inclination to inculcate in them the 'right' idea about fairness and respect. But how this is best done and whether the methods chosen have the intended impact depends on the perspectives and experiences of the young people on the receiving end. The good intentions of teachers, youth and community workers, community police officers and others responsible for initiating these activities may not be matched by the impact on young people.

This research looks at five case study projects from the perspectives of young participants. Two are educational and delivered as part of citizenship education in schools, 'Show Racism the Red Card' in Stafford – run by a police officer – and 'You, Me and Us' in Peterborough – run by the local authority's youth service. Tower Hamlets Summer University is a voluntary sector, informal education project. The 'Diversity Awareness Programme' for convicted racially motivated offenders is run by probation officers. The Jubilee Football Tournament was run by two housing associations and could be described as a community cohesion project. This research considers how young people who have been involved in the five projects see and understand racism, and their opinions about it. The research also considers the impact of the projects on their attitudes and behaviour, again from the perspectives of the young people themselves.

Methodologies

For each case study, a specific approach was devised that would best elicit the views of the young people on race and racism and, more specifically, their opinions of the effectiveness of the activity they had participated in. For each case study, the research approach used is described in detail in the relevant chapter.

In all, more than 600 young people took part in this research. The majority of these were the 11- and 12-year-old boys and girls surveyed in the schools in Stafford and Peterborough. Some comparative findings have been drawn from these relatively large datasets. The approach in the other three case studies was qualitative and involved much smaller numbers of young people. The fieldwork for these case studies included discussions in focus groups and semi-structured and in-depth interviews. The material generated by these qualitative methods allowed for a deeper exploration of some of the issues from the perspective of young people involved in the programme or project.

Structure of the report

The five projects looked at in detail are set out in Chapters 1 to 5. For each case study, the local context is described. This is followed by a short description of the programme or activity. The research approach used is then described. The main body of each case study is in two parts, both set out thematically from the perspectives of young people. The first section sets out young people's views on race and racism; which racial groups some respondents admitted to disliking and a full description of the reasons why. The second section of the case study considers the impact of the project against the backdrop of young people's thoughts and opinions. Each case study ends with a summary. The final chapter is a thematic overview of the findings of the research and their implications for future initiatives to challenge and change the views and behaviour of young people about race and racism. Throughout the report, young people's quotes are given in their own spelling. All names of people have been removed or fictionalised. No names are given for the schools in Peterborough and Stafford and the names of the neighbourhoods where the Jubilee Football Tournament took place have been fictionalised. Anonymity has thereby been maintained for those who participated in the research.

1 'Show Racism the Red Card', Stafford

Local context

Stafford is a market town in the Midlands that has not received many migrants from outside the UK since the war. In the 2001 census, 97 per cent of local residents identify themselves as white, 1 per cent as mixed, 1 per cent as Asian or Asian British and 0.5 per cent as black or black British. Eighty per cent defined themselves as Christian and less than half a per cent as Muslim. Against this backdrop of small black and minority ethnic communities and little recent inward migration, young people living or going to school in Stafford may not have had much first-hand experience of cultural or religious diversity.

'Show Racism the Red Card' programme

'Show Racism the Red Card' is an anti-racist charity, established in 1996, which seeks to combat racism by presenting professional footballers as anti-racist role models in education, for example Rio Ferdinand and Arsene Wenger have been involved. Footballers describe on video their experiences of being racially harassed. The accompanying education packs suggest brainstorming and role-playing activities for facilitators working with young people on dealing with racial harassment and racism more generally. Educational resources include videos, CD-ROMs, posters, magazines and pin badges.

The ethnic minorities liaison officer from the local police division in Stafford uses the video to work with Year 7s (11 to12 year olds). The relative absence of cultural diversity in the town means that classes of between 25 and 30 pupils usually contain fewer than three pupils from minority ethnic backgrounds. The aim is to use the video and subsequent discussion to raise awareness and stimulate critical thinking about racism, discrimination and prejudice, as well as about the experiences of black and minority ethnic people. The project complements the students' PHSE/ citizenship curriculum.

The police officer negotiates permission from schools to run the programme. Typically, at least one member of staff with an active interest in anti-racism has to champion 'Show Racism the Red Card' in order to secure agreement to run the programme. Some schools in the area are not willing to participate.

The session lasts one hour and begins with the police officer leading a discussion of race, racism, prejudice and discrimination. A five-minute section of the video is then shown. Football players and managers describe and discuss experiences of racism, ranging from racist remarks made by fans to being stopped and searched without justification by the police. The issues raised by the video are then discussed. The police officer outlines what to do and who to contact if anyone feels they are being racially victimised by a police officer. The students then individually write down what they think 'prejudice', 'discrimination' and 'racism' mean. They also do role-playing exercises in small groups. Each group is given one of the situations described in the video and asked to write on a flipchart sheet how they would feel if they had been in a similar situation.

Research approach

Researchers conducted workshops during February and March 2003 in which young people completed questionnaires with open-ended questions exploring their views about the area they lived in; the communities that lived there and relationships between them; their understandings of prejudice, discrimination and racism; their experiences of racist bullying; and their thoughts about 'Show Racism the Red Card'. Questions from the survey are in Appendix 1 to this report. Researchers were on hand for informal individual and group discussions while the questionnaires were being completed by the pupils. Of the 156 young people who completed the questionnaires, 48 per cent were boys and 51 per cent were girls. Sixty-two per cent were 12 years old; 35 per cent were 11. Most of the young people who completed the questionnaires were white. A few described themselves as black, Muslim, Asian, Chinese or mixed race.

Young people's opinions

Racism was understood as being nasty to other people because of their skin colour, religion or country of origin

In response to the question, 'What is racism?', 65 per cent of responses contained a reference to being nasty to somebody because of their skin colour or because they were black. Other issues mentioned included religion (17 per cent), country of origin (nine out of 156, 6 per cent), accent (five out of 156, 3 per cent). Eight of the responses mentioned specifically that racism meant white people are the perpetrators of unfair treatment and black or 'coloured' people are the victims (see Figure 1).

Nearly all the young people understood that being nasty to people because they were different was wrong, but almost a quarter admitted to disliking certain groups

Ninety-six per cent said it was wrong to treat people badly because they were different.

Nevertheless, around three-quarters of the young people (more girls than boys, see below) thought some groups were disliked by others in Stafford and 24 per cent admitted to disliking particular communities themselves. These figures suggest that a substantial proportion of young people thought that disliking people from other racial backgrounds was more prevalent in others than in themselves. Twenty-four per cent also thought that there were too many people from different communities living in England. Apparently negative, probably prejudiced, views about particular groups can be maintained alongside a general belief in the wrongness of unequal treatment. The young people who expressed this apparently paradoxical view may have felt that they could hold negative opinions without them affecting their subsequent behaviour towards members of that group. Alternatively they felt, although their views might be negative, they were nevertheless accurate and therefore justified behaviour that might be regarded as unfair. Perhaps the most plausible explanation is that people – young and old – can persist in apparently contradictory beliefs.

Girls are more likely than boys to point to their

Figure 1 Respondents' answer to the question, 'What is racism?', in Stafford

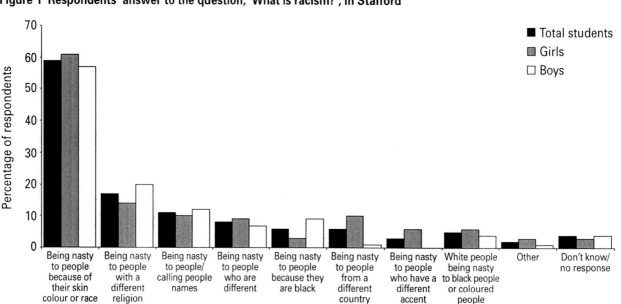

perception of dislike and unfair treatment by others – 85 per cent of girls as against 68 per cent of boys. Consistent with that more frequent sensitivity to intolerance in girls, significantly more boys expressed dislikes of other groups than girls. Thirty-two per cent of boys said they disliked certain communities and 36 per cent thought there were too many people from different communities living in England. By contrast, 16 per cent of girls said they disliked certain groups and 14 per cent said they thought there were too many people from different groups living in England (see Figures 2–5).

Figure 2 **Do you think that any of the different groups of people are disliked by other groups of people in Stafford?**

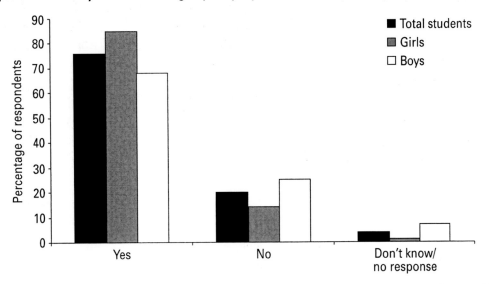

Figure 3 **Do you think there are 'too many different people from different racial communities in England?' or 'a good mix of different people from different racial communities in England?'**

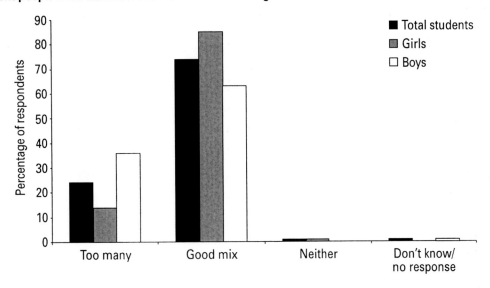

Figure 4 Are there any particular racial communities or groups of people that you dislike?

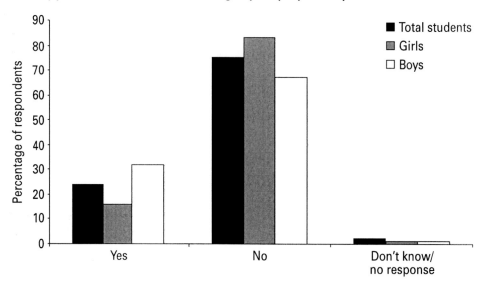

Figure 5 Do you think it is okay to dislike or call people names because they happen to be a different colour, religion or from another country than you?

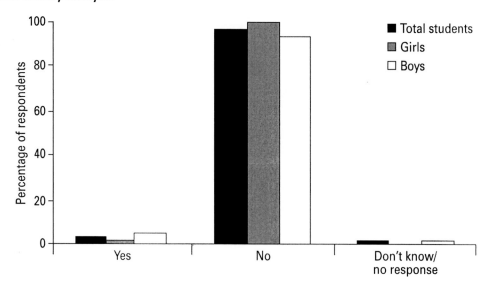

Young people disliked Asian groups more than others, but thought other people disliked black people more than others

Asked a general question about which groups were disliked by other groups in Stafford, 39 per cent of the young people mentioned black people. They also mentioned groups such as Asian, including 'Muslim', 'Pakistani', 'Asian' and 'Indian'. The mingling of racial and religious identities is a recurring theme in several case studies in this report and is the subject of comment in the findings

in Chapter 6 (see Figure 6).

When the young people were asked if they thought there were too many different communities in England, Asian people featured more prominently in the responses than black people. Seventeen per cent of the young people said they thought there were too many people from at least one Asian group in England, compared with 6 per cent who said they thought there were too many black people. Similarly, 10 per cent of the young people said they disliked people from an

Figure 6 Which groups of people are most disliked in Stafford

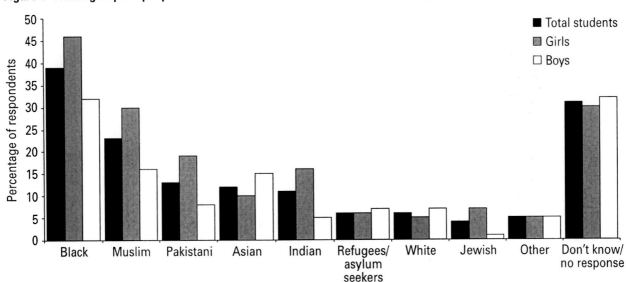

Figure 7 Are there any particular racial communities or groups of people that you dislike? If yes, what racial communities or groups of people do you dislike?

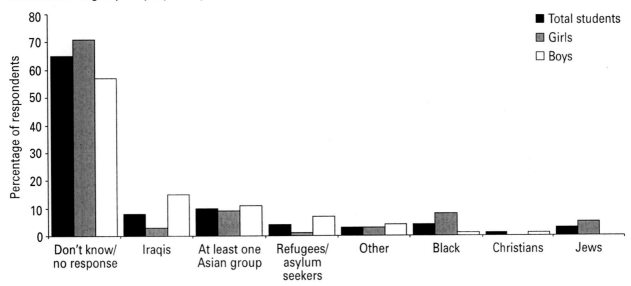

Asian community, while 4 per cent said they didn't like black people. Girls were more likely to admit to a dislike of black people than boys. For Asian people, the numbers of boys and girls who said they disliked them were roughly equal. As already noted, there are few members of any minority ethnic community living in Stafford, though more are Asian than black. Of the 1.5 per cent of census respondents who described themselves as Asian or black, there were twice as many who mentioned a South Asian identity than those who mentioned a black identity (see Figure 7).

Iraq, Afghanistan, weapons of mass destruction and the attacks on the USA, 11 September 2001
Some young people were influenced by their perceptions of the wars in Afghanistan and Iraq, as well as the political and media debate about weapons of mass destruction, al Qaeda and the attacks on the World Trade Centre and the

Pentagon on 11 September 2001. Many of the young people said they disliked Iraqis for a combination of these reasons, often rather poorly understood, grouping Iraqis and al Qaeda and labelling them responsible for the events of 11 September, as the following quotes illustrate. The quotes below are answers to the questions who do you dislike and why? The gender of the young person and the description they gave of their own racial identity are given in brackets.

> the eraceys and asuman binlanden – because of
> September 11 and war.
> ('I am white and taned', male)

In one response, the French footballer of Algerian descent, Zinedine Zidane, appears to have been confused with Saddam Hussein:

> Bin laden folloners, Zidane Husain – because they are
> causing death and making weapons for no reason.
> ('White quarter scotish 3/4 English', male)

Negative attitudes to Asians and/or Muslims as potential terrorists or enemies in war
These reasons for dislike were not confined to Iraqis, but sometimes extended to Asians and Muslims in general. Again, the young person quoted below was responding to the question 'which groups did they dislike and why?':

> Pakies – because they are going to war and killed lots
> of people.
> ('White and British', female)

One young person links concerns about weapons of mass destruction with a wider 'clash of civilisations' theme when giving his reasons for disliking Iraqis and Muslims and Asians in general:

> Terrorists from Irak and Pakistan – because they
> experiment different weapons of mass distrucksion
> and hate our way of life.
> ('English, don't really believe in a religion, white',
> male)

One young person applied a similar rationale to people from Afghanistan:

> Afghans – Because they hijack planes and kill people.
> ('White', male)

'Minority groups are not entitled to be in the UK'
Several comments suggest that a number of young people believe that certain groups are not entitled to live in the UK. One young person expressed a more general feeling that people from other racial backgrounds were trying to sneak in when they had no entitlement to be resident in the UK:

> Muzlims, Indians, pakistans Iraquies – Because they
> have there own country and they try to sneak in our
> country (theres to many).
> ('ENGLISH! White', male)

One young person acknowledged that there may be reasons why people need to escape from other countries, but that did not necessarily give them the right to live in the UK, because they bore some responsibility for the situation they had created:

> Afghanistan people – Because their in our country
> and escaping the war they created.
> ('White', male)

'Minority groups get preferential treatment'
Some linked the idea that minority groups have their own country and shouldn't be in the UK to a belief that ethnic minorities received more than their entitlement and more than white people. One young person, for example, said he disliked:

> Pakistanis, Muslims, Indians, Iraquis – because they
> do nothing at all for our country and get free housing,
> food and they have there own country.
> ('English [white] christian', male)

'Minority groups don't comply with the accepted norms of British society'
Some young people said they disliked certain groups because they broke the law or didn't obey

rules or conventions, perhaps because they came from somewhere else and either didn't know or didn't respect the accepted way of doing things in Britain. One person said he disliked Pakistani people and other illegal immigrants for this reason:

> *Illegal immigrants and pakistans – brake the law and don't obey the rules over here.*
> ('White, England', male)

Hostile or unfriendly behaviour by minority groups
Many young people said they disliked people from Asian communities because of their perceived hostile or unfriendly behaviour:

> *I am not that keen on idians because they give you evil looks, they look at you in a horrible way.*
> ('Black come from England', female)

> *I am not that keen on pakistanies – Because they are vishious.*
> ('I am coloured and my mum is white', female)

Disliking difference
Some young people said they disliked certain groups simply because other people were different in various ways:

> *coloured people ... are diffent from us.*
> ('I am white and newcastle-under-lyme', female)

One boy specified that he disliked the different way of talking:

> *different country people ... speak different then us.*
> ('normal colour, Christian', male)

Another gave differences in religious practices as a reason for dislike:

> *Musim[s] ... pray a loot and I don't*
> ('I come from England', male)

Sources of negative attitudes
The questions did not explicitly search for the sources of these attitudes, but some possibilities are nevertheless suggested by the responses. The link between Muslims, Asians, refugees and asylum seekers in the UK and terrorism and war seems to be influenced by media stories. The survey was taken in the period leading up to the invasion of Iraq when media coverage and public discussion was extensive. The interpretation of media stories might either be relayed or mediated by parents or peers. Some young people drew attention to the influence of their family on their opinions. One young white girl said she disliked Jews because she was 'brout up like that'. Personal experiences of individuals from minority groups have also led to a more general dislike of the entire group:

> *Muslim and arab – Because they lie, cheat and are extremely horrible to you. You cannot trust them. They HAVE done this to me for a long time.*
> ('British', male)

Young people had a poor sense of their own identity but a strong grasp of which different groups lived in their town
Some young people struggled to describe their racial identity without multiple-choice options or prompts. Many found it one of the hardest questions on the questionnaire. Many respondents replied with comments like 'tall' or 'fat' or 'blond hair, brown eyes', for example. In some instances, descriptions were precise and individual, unrelated to conventional adult group identities, for example, 'Newcastle-under-Lyme', 'quarter Scottish'.

When asked about the racial communities that live in Stafford, the respondents most commonly drew the distinction between Muslims and others. Nationality (particularly in the case of Asian people and people from Wales, Scotland and Ireland, the USA and European countries) was another common form of categorisation. Religion (specifying Christianity and several religions associated with Asia) and skin colour (in the case of black people) were also mentioned. Some groups were identified by status (refugees) or their heritage (mixed race, 'gypsies') (see Figure 8).

Figure 8 Respondents' awareness of other groups in Stafford

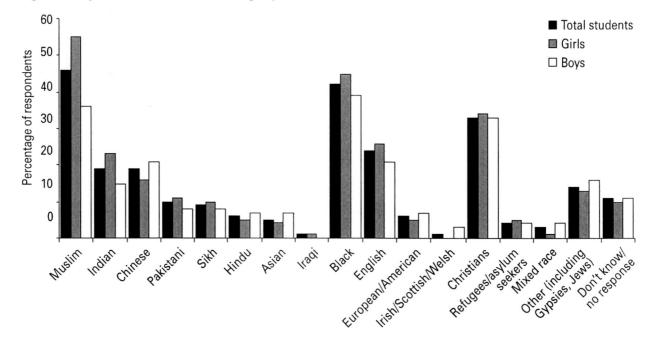

The presence of the groups most commonly mentioned – Indians, Pakistanis and black – are confirmed by census data.

Limited understanding of cultural differences
Responses to a question about religious symbols suggests limited detailed knowledge about cultural differences. While nearly all of the respondents recognised the Christian symbol, only a minority recognised symbols associated with Islam, Judaism and Sikhism, such as the Star of David or the crescent of Islam. This did not vary significantly with gender (see Figures 9 and 10).

Impact of 'Show Racism the Red Card'

See Figures 11 and 12 for what respondents in Stafford learnt from 'Show Racism the Red Card' and how they thought and felt differently after the project.

The majority of participants enjoyed the programme
Seventy-two per cent of the young people said they enjoyed 'Show Racism the Red Card', while 22 per

cent said they did not and a further nine of the 156 participants (6 per cent) either did not respond or said they didn't know. Fifteen per cent said their favourite session was making a poster; 14 per cent said watching the video; 12 per cent said the best thing was understanding more about racism; 10 per cent said the role-play activities and 11 of the 156 (7 per cent – mostly boys) said seeing famous footballers talk about their experiences of racism (particularly Rio Ferdinand) was their favourite session. Other sessions also gained approval from smaller proportions of young people. There was more of a consensus about the aspects they disliked: 47 per cent said they didn't like hearing about people getting picked on or experiencing racism.

Reinforced messages and a more nuanced understanding
The responses of 79 per cent of the young people suggested they had gained a more in-depth understanding of racism, or some of their knowledge of racism being wrong had been reinforced. Fifty-eight per cent responded in a

Figure 9 Religious symbols used in questionnaire

Figure 10 Respondents' awareness of religious symbols in Stafford

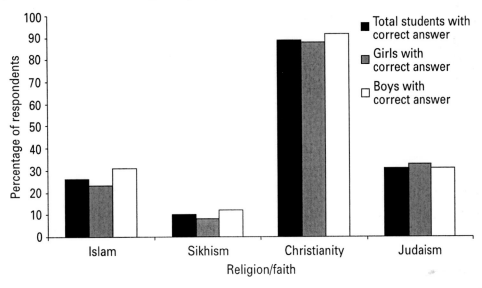

Figure 11 What respondents in Stafford learnt from 'Show Racism the Red Card'

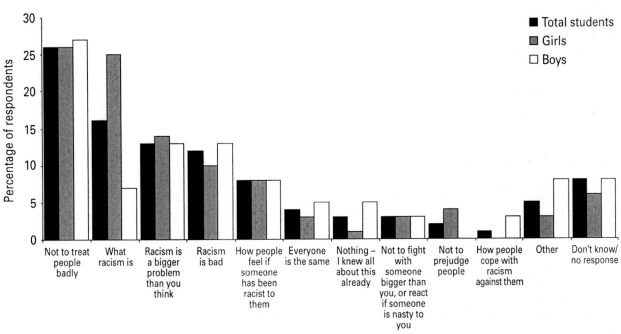

Figure 12 How respondents in Stafford responded to the question, 'Do you think that the video and activities have made you think and feel differently about people who may be a different colour or religion from you?'

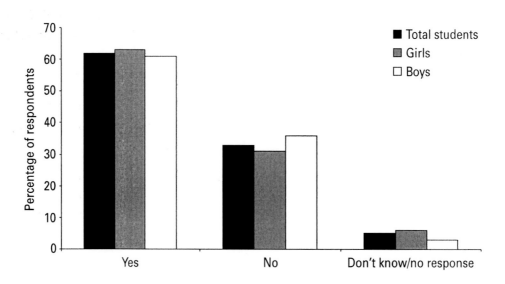

similar way to the question asking whether they thought or felt differently as a result of the programme. One person commented that they didn't feel any differently but had learnt more about racism:

it made me know a bit more about it not made me feel differently.
('White quarter scotish 3/4 english', male)

Twenty-six per cent said they had learnt not to treat people badly. One young person said they had learnt:

don't call black people names!
('am good', male)

Sixteen per cent said they knew more about what racism and other concepts meant:

what racism, predjuce + discrimination means.
('english/African', female)

I learned alot more about racism.
('White/English', female)

Thirteen per cent said they had learnt that racism was a bigger problem than they had been aware of:

I learnt that there is more racism in the world than you think.
('white, English', female)

Twelve per cent said they had learnt that racism was bad:

racism is a bad thing to do.
('British-white', female)

racism is a crime.
('English', male)

Twelve people said they had a better understanding of how people feel as a result of racial abuse:

that bullying people make them feel really sad and that knowone should be mean.
('I am white', male)

Six people said they had learnt that everyone is the same. The two responses set out below were given by people of different racial backgrounds:

just because there black ther still the same.
('white', male)

we are all the same and no one is different.
('I am a muslim and I am brown', female)

Seventeen per cent said they now felt that people who were racially or culturally different were, beneath the superficial differences, the same as them:

> not to pick on people because we are all the same we are humans.
> ('Christianity', female)

> that its what inside that counts.
> ('christian', female)

Seventeen per cent also said they felt that people should be nice to people who are different, or that it is nasty to be horrible to them. Twelve per cent said they felt sorry for people who suffered from racial harassment or abuse. One person referred to the death of Stephen Lawrence:

> the boy got killed just because he was a different colour.
> ('white', male)

'I already knew all this'

Twenty-one per cent of the respondents said that they did not think or feel any differently as a result of the programme because they were not racist anyway. Five people said they didn't learn anything for similar reasons:

> I learnt nothing (because I already knew it).
> ('half Irish half English', female)

> I already felt that rasism in nasty.
> ('British, white, no religion', female)

> I already thought that people of a different religion or colour are the same as anyone else.
> ('white, English', female)

'Nothing will change the way I feel'

Three of the young people said that the programme had not influenced their negative attitudes:

> nothing will change how I feel about it!
> ('English [white] christian', male)

One person's comment suggests the influence of the media's portrayal of world events:

> I still felt the same because I don't think its right to blow up the wold trade centre and have chemical weapons.
> ('I am white and taned', male)

Similarly, one young person suggests that she doesn't have a problem with black people, but Iraq is a different matter:

> because I think that black people are the same as white people. But everyone doesn't like Iraq because we don't know if he is hiding weapons.
> ('mixed race', female)

A small number of comments suggest that some young people drew more worrying conclusions from the programme. For example, one young person said he had learnt:

> that police can't control pakistans.
> ('ENGLISH! white', male)

Another said that, as a result of the programme, she now felt:

> that if they were not in this contry there would no be as much troble.
> ('browny, bloney hair, blue eyes, ugly', female)

Dealing with racism and standing up for others

Four people said they had learnt not to fight with someone bigger than themselves or to retaliate if someone racially abused them. Two people said they felt more likely to stick up for someone else:

> that if a person that I don't know is a different religion or colour to them and some people were bullying them, I would stick up for them and to never bully someone cause its wrong!
> ('white', female)

Summary

'Show Racism the Red Card' is clearly structured, planned and delivered. Young people enjoy the programme and the range of activities in it. It has had a beneficial impact on young people's understanding of racial prejudice and racist behaviour. The programme has also reinforced the idea that racism is wrong. Less impact has been made on encouraging young people to challenge racist behaviour in others. Little impact appears to have been made on the specific issues raised by the opinions and prejudices of young people set out above. Nor have the young people apparently taken on the important message that information received from whatever source might usefully be questioned and examined before being accepted. A small number of young people appear to have stuck to entrenched racist views despite participating in 'Show Racism the Red Card'. The programme seems to have done less to address young people's own concerns and those issues, such as Iraq, they regard as being of contemporary relevance.

2 'You, Me and Us', Peterborough

Local context

Ninety per cent of Peterborough's residents are white British people, however the city is also home to significant minority communities – 7 per cent of the people who live there identified themselves as Asian or Asian British in the 2001 census. Five per cent said they were Pakistani and 2 per cent said they were Indian. Six per cent described themselves as Muslim. One per cent identified themselves as Black or Black British and 2 per cent said they had a mixed heritage.

The mix of communities has further grown as a result of the city becoming a cluster area for the dispersal of asylum seekers by the Home Office in 2000. More than a thousand people arrived in the city between 2000 and 2002. The City Council manages accommodation through the National Asylum Seekers Support dispersal programme for people from over 40 countries who speak more than 23 languages. In addition, a substantial Portuguese community has come to live in the town since 2001, attracted by agricultural employment in East Anglia.

Tensions have surfaced following the murder in 2001 of Ross Parker, a white young man. Three young Asian men were subsequently convicted. Youth workers commented that the arrival of asylum seekers and Portuguese people has also created tension.

'You, Me and Us' programme

'You, Me and Us' is run with Year 7 students (11 to 12 year olds) in all 13 high schools in Peterborough. The programme is designed to complement the PHSE/citizenship curriculum. The project is co-ordinated by the Youth Action Against Crime Unit of the local authority. Workshops are delivered by a police community safety liaison officer, a representative from the Race Equality Council, the local authority's multicultural education officer, members of the youth offending team, a detached youth worker and drama students from the local college. Seven workshops are held during one school day. Depending on the structure of the day and size of the school, pupils are likely to attend four out of the seven workshops. Drama, poetry, storytelling, music and art are all part of the programme's activities.

'You, Me and Us' seeks to raise awareness, reduce racism and encourage reporting of racist behaviour, bullying and intolerance. It also seeks to encourage pupils to 'challenge prejudice and hatred wherever it is found'. In addition, activities seek to 'get students interested in, rather than afraid of, sameness and difference, and to get across the message that you need both "you" and "me" to make "us"' and thereby to 'encourage young people to think in new ways about themselves and their place in the world'.

Research approach

With the help of the youth worker who co-ordinates the programme, researchers took part in 'You, Me and Us' in three schools in Peterborough in February and March 2003. Two of the schools were in central Peterborough and had significant numbers of minority ethnic pupils (Schools 1 and 2 in the figures). The third school was outside the city centre and had far fewer minority ethnic pupils (School 3 in the figures). The usual programme of workshops was varied to include a session conducted by researchers in which young people completed a questionnaire exploring their views about the area they lived in; the communities that lived there and relationships between them; their understandings of prejudice, discrimination and racism; and their experiences of racist bullying. This questionnaire was similar, though not quite identical, to the first half of the one used in Stafford. Young people completed the questionnaire individually, assisted by a researcher clarifying queries and responding to concerns.

While the young people were encouraged to give individual answers, discussion in small groups may have influenced the responses given. Two-hundred-and-sixty-eight young people completed the first questionnaire exploring attitudes and understandings. They were either 11 or 12 years of age and there was a roughly equal number of male and female pupils.

Researchers returned to the same three schools in March and April 2003 to administer a second questionnaire to pupils in classes that had participated in 'You, Me and Us'. The second questionnaire explored views about 'You, Me and Us' and was completed by 394 students in a larger number of classes than the first questionnaire. This larger group included virtually all the young people who had filled in the first questionnaire. The others had attended 'You, Me and Us' but were in classes in which the first questionnaire had not been conducted on the first visit. The questions used in both research instruments are given in the Appendices. This two-stage approach to the research was different from the survey conducted in Stafford. In that case, a single visit was made by researchers to the school and the attitudinal questions were included in a single questionnaire along with questions about the impact of 'Show Racism the Red Card'.

Young people's opinions

Racism is understood as being nasty to other people because of their skin colour, religion or because of their country of origin

Most respondents' definition of racism suggested they saw it as treating people badly because they were different. Differences that some young people felt might lead to unfair treatment were not confined to skin colour, but also included religion, country of origin, language, accent and other cultural differences such as clothes or names. Only one of the young people surveyed in the two schools in which this question was asked

specifically said that racism was something perpetrated by white people. By contrast in Stafford, with its much less multiracial community than in Peterborough, more young people saw racism as white people treating black people badly (see Figure 13).

Nearly half admitted to disliking certain groups, although nearly all respondents understood that being nasty to people because they were different is wrong

Ninety-two per cent of the respondents in Peterborough (compared to three-quarters in Stafford) felt some communities in the town were disliked by other groups, although 63 per cent thought there was a good mix, suggesting that, as in Stafford, many respondents felt that other people were more likely to have these dislikes than themselves. This perhaps reflects a caution about admitting to personal prejudice or dislike in a survey, while being willing to impersonally acknowledge it in others. The greater awareness of other people's perceived intolerance in Peterborough perhaps reflects the relatively high profile of concerns about race in the local media and the more diverse community in the city.

A much smaller, but nevertheless significant, proportion expressed reservations about diversity in the town and admitted to negative views about other communities there: 28 per cent of respondents felt that there were too many people from different racial communities in Peterborough and 43 per cent said they disliked certain racial communities. More boys than girls thought there were too many people from different racial communities in Peterborough, but more girls than boys said they disliked people from different racial groups. The gender difference is significant, but, nevertheless, intolerance is evidently not the preserve of boys, as also noted in Stafford. Dislike of people from different groups was more marked in the two inner-city, more multiracial schools (Schools 1 and 2) than in the less diverse school outside the city centre (School 3). In the two

Figure 13 Respondents' answer to the question, 'What is racism?', in Peterborough

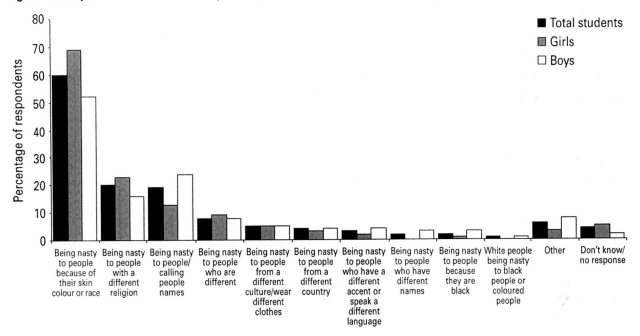

Note: this question was not asked when the questionnaire was conducted at School 1.

inner-city schools, 56 per cent and 63 per cent of respondents said they disliked certain other groups, compared with 22 per cent at the rural school. Proximity of young people from different racial backgrounds has possibly bred a greater degree of intolerance – perhaps a rather depressing finding.

Despite 43 per cent of respondents admitting that they disliked people from different communities, 93 per cent of respondents felt it was wrong to dislike or call people names because of their colour, religion or being from another country. More girls (97 per cent) than boys (87 per cent) held this view. Dislike is perhaps perceived as a permissible attitude, without legitimising aggressive behaviour. Intolerant attitudes can, some respondents seem to believe, be held onto without them growing into unfair or hostile treatment. Again similar findings came through in Stafford (see Figures 14–16).

Asian, Portuguese, asylum seekers/refugees and white communities are most likely to be seen as disliked communities or as being too numerous
Some young people cited Asian communities, and in particular people from a Pakistani or Muslim background, as being too numerous or as people they disliked. Thirty-nine (15 per cent) of the total number of responses thought there were too many Pakistani people in Peterborough, 34 (13 per cent) thought there were too many Muslims and 24 (9 per cent) thought there were too many Asians. Seventeen people (6 per cent) said they didn't like Pakistani people, ten (4 per cent) said they didn't like Asians and eight (3 per cent) said they didn't like Muslims. Other South Asian groups were also identified: 29 (11 per cent) said they thought there were too many Indians or Hindus and 15 (6 per cent) said there were too many Sikhs. Similar proportions of young people were concerned about more recent arrivals – asylum seekers and Portuguese people. Fifteen people (6 per cent) said they disliked asylum seekers or refugees and 22 (8 per cent) said they thought there were too many.

Figure 14 Do you think there are 'too many different people from different racial communities in Peterborough?' or 'a good mix of different people from different racial communities in Peterborough?' (Individual responses)

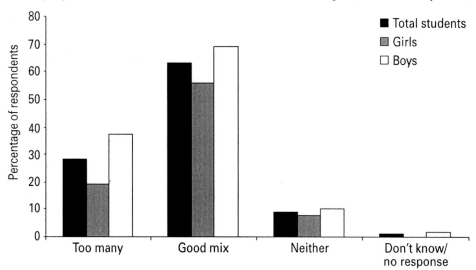

Figure 15 Are there any particular racial communities or groups of people that you dislike? (School responses)

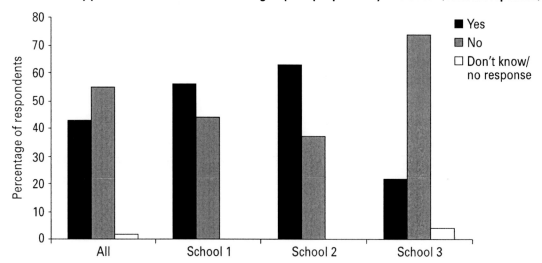

Figure 16 Are there any particular racial communities or groups of people that you dislike? (Individual responses)

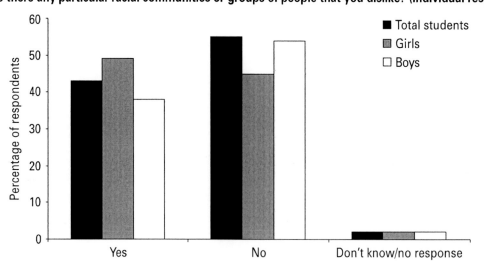

Similarly, 15 (6 per cent) said they disliked Portuguese people and 21 (8 per cent) said there were too many. Sixteen (6 per cent) of the young people said they disliked either white people or British or English people. Black (as distinct from Asian) people seemed less of a concern – 21 (8 per cent) of the young people said there were too many black people and eight (3 per cent) disliked black people. Having noted this range of dislikes, it is also important to note that between one-third and two-thirds of pupils (depending on the school) did not mention disliking any groups and felt there was a good mix (see Figures 17–19).

Figure 17 Do you think there are 'too many different people from different racial communities in Peterborough?' or 'a good mix of different people from different racial communities in Peterborough?' (School responses)

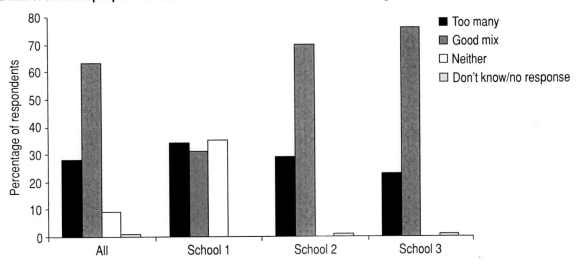

Figure 18 If you think there are too many different communities or groups of people in Peterborough which one(s) do you think there are too many of?

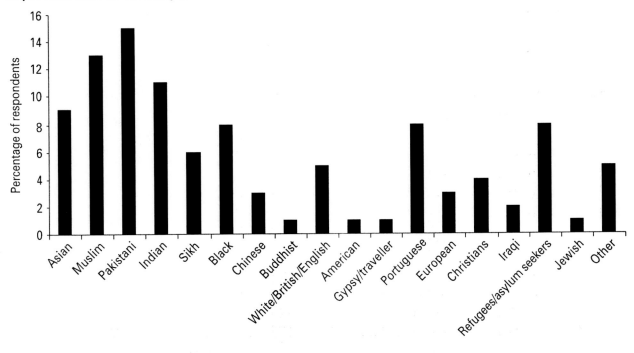

Figure 19 Are there any particular racial communities or groups of people that you dislike? If yes, what racial communities or groups of people do you dislike?

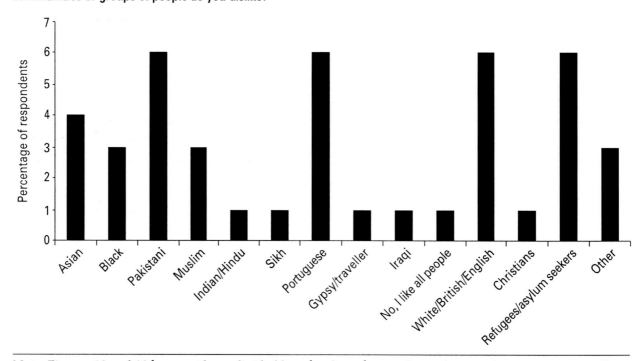

Note: Figures 18 and 19 have not been divided by schools as the numbers of respondents were too small to be statistically significant.

Reasons for dislike

The young people who said they disliked people from other groups were asked for reasons for their dislike. The themes that emerged are outlined below. A number of comments also suggest the possible sources for these attitudes. For each of the quotes that follow, the young person's gender and how they described themselves is given in brackets.

Terrorism

Although not mentioned by many young people, the dislike of some young people for Iraqis, Asians and Muslims in general was linked to terrorism. One commented:

People in Iraq ... did horrible nonforgiveable actions!
('Christian, white', female)

One young person linked terrorism to unpleasant behaviour and a sense of being overwhelmed by Asian people:

Pakistanies ... are horrible and terrorists and the fill up our country.
('white', female)

Disliking difference

Some people said they disliked people from certain groups because they were just different in various ways, as the following comments illustrate:

ASIANS ... are different.
('white', female)

Some noted difference in religion:

Buddism because of religion.
('white', male)

Sikhism – cause of there religion.
('Christianity', male)

Another young person expressed confusion at other people's difference:

Pourgenes – Because I just can't understand them. They look at you top to bottom. Most of them can't even dress up propely.
('I don't know', female)

Perceptions of too many people who belong in other countries

Several others made reference to a sense of being overwhelmed by people of different backgrounds. Some also linked this to a belief that such people belonged in other countries, as the following quotes illustrate:

Pakistan ... are invading our country.
('white, English', male)

Pakiestanis – because there in my country and theres is Pakistan.
('white', male)

One person's reasons for disliking Muslims is based on local concerns:

Muslims ... built a mosque in Peterborough.
('White, Christian', male)

Some also expressed concern about there being too many asylum seekers and refugees. One respondent commented:

Asilum seekers – there's to many of them.
('white, sorta taned', male)

The view that certain groups should not be in Britain was also extended to refugees and illegal immigrants, as the following quotes illustrate:

refugees ... did not ask permistion to come into our country.
('white', male)

elegal immigrants ... are not supose to be in a country and they are in it.
('White, Germany, Christianity', male)

A comment by one Pakistani girl suggests she feels disturbed by the arrival of refugees and other newcomers. Despite her own Pakistani background, she regarded Peterborough as 'our town':

I hate jews and refugees and portugees – Why do refugees appear in our town? There are other people that are living in the area and the disturb you.
('Pakistani', female)

Perceptions that refugees and asylum seekers get preferential treatment

Some young people justified dislike of refugees and asylum seekers on the grounds that they received better treatment than local people who had lived in Britain for longer:

asylum – Because they get everything for free, car, money, mobile phone.
('Scottish', female)

asylum seekers ... get everything and it can only take on person to speak in a different langwhich.
('christian', female)

Refregies ... they get more than us.
('I am nice and I will never say anything nasty, English', female)

Perceptions of minority groups as hostile, unpleasant or troublemakers

The behaviour of particular groups as perceived by respondents is given as justification for dislike. Several white young people, for example, said they did not like some minority or religious communities because of the way they behaved:

Most of the muslims cultures – because they always take the mick out of my couler I am white that's why.
('don't know', female)

Afghanistan ... some of them have followed and taken pictures of me.
('English', female)

One person's dislike of refugees was partly rooted in her own experience of two of them:

I don't like refugees – because I got chast by two and they look you up.
('white', female)

As already mentioned, racially motivated murder has been a subject of intense discussion among local people and in the local press. Some people linked different minority groups with murders:

Portugal – Because they kill people and pakistain kill people.
('I am white and I don't go to church', male)

England, black people and christain – because the black people killed a girl but.
('I am from Pakistan', male)

Several people also said they disliked Portuguese people because of the way they behaved:

potuges because their bad behaviour at looking starlly.
('Pakistani, Islam, I'm not nice', female)

Portuguese … are dirty nasty and greedy.
('muslim [Pakistani]', male)

Again, personal experience seems to be important:

portugius – because I had a fight with them, and they tried to kidnap my brother.
('British muslim', male)

One person linked his negative experiences of Pakistani people with their propensity to riot:

Packestan – because they don't like me, they think there hard, they call me midet and push and riot.
('Sporty, England', male)

Asian people were also mentioned by some as troublemakers, for starting fights and other kinds of anti-social behaviour:

Aishens … are always startign fights.
('English', female)

Seeks (Asians) – they cause trouble.
('white and proud, Irish cathlic', female)

Asians … are really loud they stay up really late and let their kids roam the steet when they are about 2 yrs.
('White, British, Christian', male)

Perceptions of the white majority as nasty, aggressive and racist
Several young people said they disliked English or white people because they were perceived to be nasty. This quote is typical of these views:

England – because they sword at you.
('I'm brown and I go to church. My parents are from Slovakia', male)

Some people specifically said they disliked white people (and, in the case quoted below, black people too) because they were racist:

white people/black people – cause they are racist.
('Muslim', male)

In what appears to be a reversal of the linking of Muslims and international terrorism, one Pakistani boy linked the racism of local people to global issues – his perception of the racism of the US President:

Peterborough/America – Bush is racist/They are racist.
('Muslim/Pakistani/Islamic', male)

A Pakistani boy appeared to dislike most of the racial groups in the city other than his own:

Black people and Christian – they think for much of them self. They crazy they stupid they jealouse.
('I am from Pakistan', male)

Some young Muslim people particularly singled out skinheads as the group they disliked:

skin heads – they start on you for nothing, tork about your couler.
('Muslim', male)

Others singled out the National Front:

National Fronts – Because they hate me, so, I have a right to hate them.
('I am a proud British Muslim', female)

Limited understanding of cultural differences

As in Stafford, the young people were asked to identify four religious symbols (see Figure 9 in Chapter 1). Over 90 per cent recognised the Christian symbol, and over 60 per cent recognised both Jewish and Islamic symbols. The Sikh symbol was least well recognised. In the school that had the highest numbers of Pakistani and Muslim students (School 2), nearly 90 per cent of participants recognised the Islamic symbol. The responses of boys and girls were not distinctly different (see Figures 20 and 21). Although multicultural schools may not be more tolerant, on this evidence, the pupils that attend them are more knowledgeable about other religions.

Impact of 'You, Me and Us'

Three-hundred-and-ninety-four young people completed the second questionnaire exploring attitudes to the project itself.

Figure 20 Respondents' awareness of religious symbols in Peterborough (all schools)

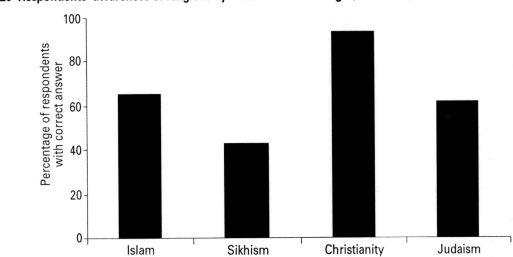

Figure 21 Respondents' awareness of religious symbols in Peterborough (individual school responses)

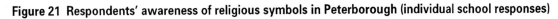
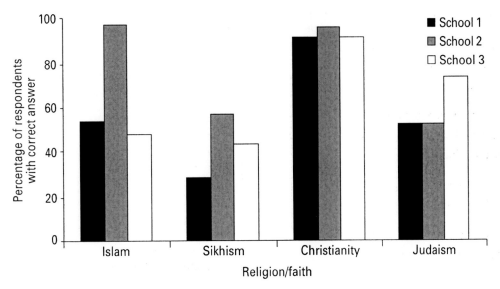

The overwhelming majority of participants enjoyed 'You, Me and Us'

Ninety-three per cent of the young people said they enjoyed 'You, Me and Us', 7 per cent said they didn't. When asked why, 65 per cent said because it was fun, enjoyable or exciting. Twenty-six per cent said they enjoyed it specifically because it was educational or informative. The comment below is typical:

> because it taught us alot and it was trendy. Don't bully people.
> ('I'm white', female)

A further 25 per cent of young people who were asked said they enjoyed it because it was better than ordinary school lessons or that it meant they could get out of lessons for a day:

> because often in school we just write and it gets bored doing it again + again.
> ('Islam, England', female)

Eleven per cent liked it particularly because the presenters were good, funny, friendly and/or helpful. Eighteen people (5 per cent) said they didn't like some of the workshops, ten (3 per cent) said they thought it was boring and six (2 per cent) said there was too much work to do. One young person who missed the event suggests a measure of its popularity:

> I wasn't here but my friends told me that it was so much fun so I want the same to happen when Im in school except the poetry they said it was boring.
> ('I'm wite and I'm Lithuanian I have blue eye and blond hair', female)

Most aspects of the programme went down well but some of the workshops were particularly popular. Forty per cent of the students said they enjoyed the drama workshop most. Thirty-four per cent said they liked the singing workshop and 22 per cent placed storytelling top of their list of preferences. Twenty-six (7 per cent) said they couldn't differentiate – they liked all of it. When asked which workshops they disliked the most, respondents showed significant disapproval of only two sessions – 19 per cent responded that they didn't like the poetry workshop and 14 per cent said they didn't like the session where they had to complete the questionnaires for this research. Twenty-nine per cent responded that they didn't dislike any of it (see Figures 22–27).

Figure 22 Respondents' reactions to 'You, Me and Us'

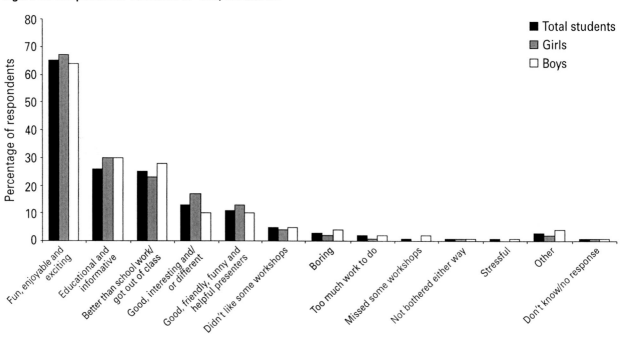

Figure 23 What respondents felt they learnt from 'You, Me and Us'

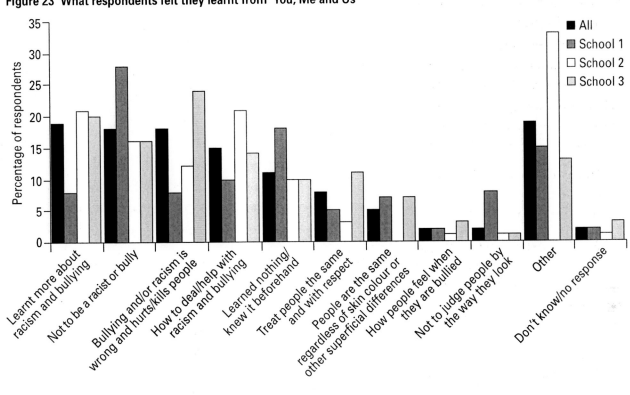

Figure 24 Whether respondents felt differently about racism after 'You, Me and Us'

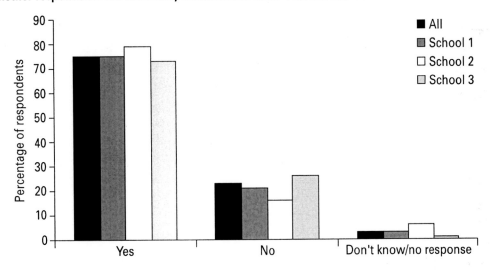

Figure 25 Ways in which respondents felt differently about racism after 'You, Me and Us'

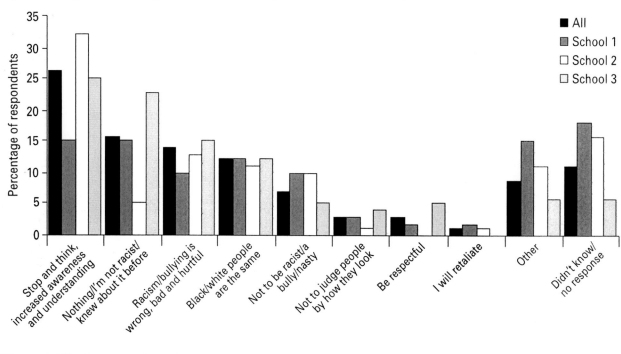

Figure 26 Whether respondents behaved differently after 'You, Me and Us'

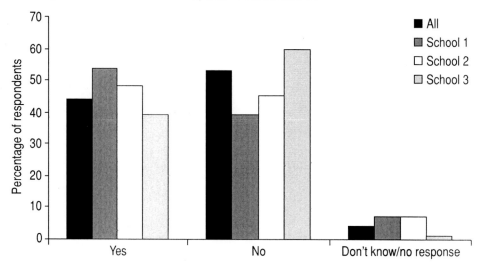

Figure 27 Ways in which respondents behaved differently after 'You, Me and Us'

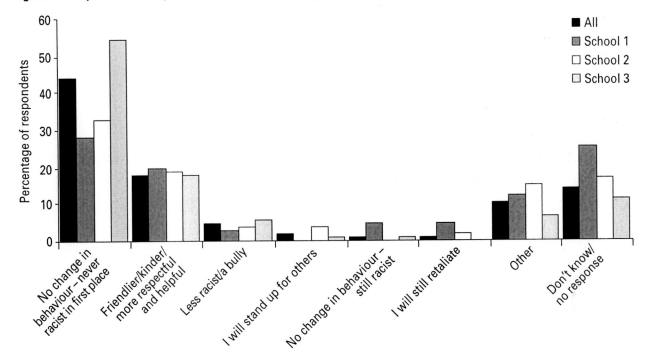

'I already knew all this'

When asked if they behaved differently, 44 per cent said they did not because they were not racist in the first place:

because I was never racist.
('White ennglish ½ irish catlic', male)

because I was NEVER racist.
('British', female)

A further 16 per cent said that they didn't feel any differently after the programme for similar reasons:

No! because I already a good girl.
('Islam, England', female)

because it was just the same things again and again and i allready know them.
('Pakistani/British', male)

Eleven per cent of the young people said that they didn't learn anything because they had encountered all the issues raised or because they weren't bullies anyway:

I learned not to bully people, well I don't anyway.
(No response to gender or identity question)

In responses to these questions, other influences can be inferred, including formal education, the media, family and friends:

I didn't learn anything because I learnt it all in primary school.
('mixed race', female)

'I say this because I have watched plenty of T.V. Documentry series about racism.
('English, white', male)

because before YOU-ME-US came I all ready learnt about this stuff from my mum + Dad.
('I'm English, [white]', female)

One response countered the view already quoted that racism and discrimination had been discussed earlier in the school career:

it has made me think different because we dont learn much about it in school so I didnt really understand much about it.
('White, English, British', female)

Familiarity with friends or family members from different backgrounds was given as a source of learning about racism:

I was already nice to other religons. One of my best friends is from a different background.
('White/English', male)

I have had a black friend since nursery school so I already knew that name calling could affect him.
('English, white', male)

because I have black/coloured people in my family, and I think highly of them!!!
('I was born in South Africa! I am a bit brown', female)

because I not racid because my dads family is half cast & because sum of my mates are aisan.
('¼ cast my dad is half cast', female)

Reinforced messages and a more nuanced understanding

A number of young people suggested that they had a better understanding of the complexities and subtleties of racism and cultural difference after 'You, Me and Us'. Many responses also suggested that positive messages had been reinforced. For example, when asked what they had learnt, 19 per cent said they had learnt more about racism or bullying. The responses of a further 18 per cent suggested they had specifically learnt that bullying and / or racism is wrong, that it can hurt people and sometimes leads to deaths:

I learnt that everyone is different but it is not nice to pick on other.
('English, christain white', female)

I learnt that racism kills people sometimes if it gets really bad.
('my mum comes from Thailand', female)

that loads of people die every year from bullying.
('[White] English', female)

Similarly, 26 per cent said they thought differently and had gained a better understanding of the extent of racism from 'You, Me and Us':

it has made me think differently because I never realised people that are differnt skin colour are treated so bad.
('I do not have any religion', female)

One boy began to question the acceptability of racist jokes:

its made me think differently about racist jokes.
('I am English and I'm white', male)

One girl seemed to have gained empathy with those who experienced racism and that had led her to a moral conclusion:

I learnt what the person feels like and that no-one likes it. I didn't bully or be racist before but now I understand why it's wrong.
('White, Christian, Parents from England', female)

Another boy noted the impact of racism and bullying on others:

this time it really went into the effects of bullying and racism.
('White, no religion, normal, England/Thailand', male)

Some of the responses suggested that not all the messages had been understood as intended. For example, the day began with a discussion about football hats and scarves, with an implicit message about not making decisions about other people based on stereotypes. One young person, however, seems to have come to a slightly different conclusion, saying he had learnt:

that you are racist just by booing some ones hat.
('British', male)

Changing behaviour for the better

A number of responses suggest that 'You, Me and Us' had a positive impact on some young people's attitudes and previous racially motivated behaviour. The following two comments suggest that some young people learnt that you could be hurtful without knowing:

I learn't you could bully someone without even nowing you are and that even if you don't mean too. And bullying isn't just verbally.
('White, chrission, England', female)

Acknowledging widespread bullying had made one young man take a closer look at his own behaviour:

I learnt that bullying occurs everywhere and sometimes you are like a bully.
('brown, Muslim', male)

Thirty (8 per cent) of the young people said they had learnt that people should be treated the same and with respect, and a further 19 (5 per cent) said that they had learnt that people should be treated the same regardless of skin colour or other superficial differences:

I learnt that people should be treated the same and respect.
('OK, fine thanx [British]', male)

I learnt people are all different, but you should treat everyone the same.
('white', female)

One girl seems to have received a positive message about the acceptability of being different:

that everyone has a right to have a good time wherever they are, whoever they are and whatever they look like.
('skin = white, religion = Ukrainian Catholic', female)

Others also took away a positive message about equality despite superficial difference:

I learnt that all people are equal.
('I am white and from England', male)

I learned that just because your coloured dos'nt mean your different.
('I am a different religion, coloured', female)

I learnt that everybody may look and sound different but they are just like us inside.
('English, white skin colour', female)

One young person's response suggests that he has learnt that he shouldn't be racist if he wants to stay out of trouble:

how not to call anybody names like (paki, nigger, black b*****d) so you can't get into trouble.
('White, England, christian', male)

Twenty-nine (7 per cent) of the young people, in answer to the question 'Do you feel differently?', said that they were less of a bully or less racially abusive. These two comments are typical:

I do't bully people no-more.
('I'm white', female)

I used to call people names but I do not call people names any more.
(No response to identity or gender question)

Similarly, 10 per cent of the young people responded to the question 'Do you behave differently?' by noting that they were less of a bully, less racially abusive, less violent or less likely to be amused by racist jokes:

I was going to say pakie to someone but I didn't.
('I don't care It doesn't bother me', female)

stop staring at them.
('I'm chinese', female)

people sometimes told me rude jokes, I already knew how rude they are but I found them funny. Now I don't find them funny at all.
('English – white skin – christian – not at all since I was 9', male)

yes because I used to be a little bit of a bully but now that I've changed.
('I don't really come from anyther contry, British')

yes becaus I use to behave like I big headed and if you call me this Ill beat you up but if someone else beat's u up you wold lik it.
('brown, muslim, Britin', male)

A number of other young people suggested that the project had a positive impact on other people's behaviour so the programme did not need changing or improving:

no because I think that it got through to the people who were racist.
('British', female)

no because it was done very well and it changed how a lot of people treat others.
('I am a muslim a fair brown colour, mum and dad from Pakistan', female)

no because it has made a lot of people not bully
('white', female)

because some of the people I know have not been as racist.
('English', male)

Twenty (5 per cent) of the people said that there should be more programmes like 'You, Me and Us' because they worked:

because they help and they work.
('White, Ginger hair, Brown eyes, Freckles', female)

after you-me-us project left people were acting differently to each other.
('I am white, no religion and was born in England', female)

Dealing with racism and standing up for others
Fifteen per cent of the young people felt better equipped either to deal with racism themselves or intervene in some way to protect others who are suffering from it:

I learn't how I can help.
('white', male)

I learned that we should respect everyone + that telling someone if you are being bullied is the best way to resolve the problem.
('White and English', female)

I learnt about what you should do if you are being bullied. And that there are lots of choices.
('Christan', male)

Six people (2 per cent) said they had behaved differently by standing up for others:

I always help my friend who gets bullied and stick up for them.
('I am from Pakistan I have dark coloured skin and a muslim', female)

because this person was being bullied by the same person who is the same skin colour as me and I helped the person who was being bullied.
('I am muslim and my parents come from Pakistan', male)

my friend who is black was being picked on and I broke it up.
('England white', male)

it has made me think about racist people I used to think 'fine that's there opion' and I would let them get on with i. I won't now.
('white', female)

I tell my dad off every time hes racist.
('white – C of E – $\frac{1}{4}$ Chinese – $\frac{1}{16}$ welch rest English')

Racism isn't a big deal.
(No answers to identity, gender questions)

However, 32 (8 per cent) said that there should not be more programmes like 'You, Me and Us' because they were pointless and there was no need for them because racism wasn't that much of a problem:

because it's pointless when most people arn't racist.
('Athist', male)

because racism isnt a big deal here at school.
('British', male)

I say that because everything is fine
('White, aqua blue eyes, gold')

'Nothing will change the way I feel'

Some responses suggest a small hard core of young people still dislike people from other groups and behave in a racist way. Some young people said they felt no differently as a result of the programme:

it just didnt make me feel differently!
('White, English', male)

no, my opinions are still the same.
('White, English from England', female)

Similarly, a few responded that they would not behave differently:

[No] *because sometimes when your in public, people from other religions/countries just stare at you and give you dirty looks.*
('white', female)

because I don't care.
('Private!')

A few young people said that their behaviour hadn't changed because they felt it was important to retaliate:

I still call them packies and other stuff. But they still be racist to me so I am back.
('[White] English', female)

if someone calls me a name then I call them something back.
('White and I have no religion', male)

because they pick on me then I will pick on them.
('short brown hire, hazel eyes', female)

'Racism is big in Peterborough'

Twenty-five per cent of the young people felt that there should be more programmes like 'You, Me and Us' because racism was still a big concern. Some comments referred to troubling situations at their schools:

because there are a lot of nasty people in this school.
('White, Christian, England', male)

because there is a lot of racism in the school.
('I have freckles', male)

because at dinnertime you here of fights that have happened or are going to happen from the white against the coloured.
('white, don't have a religion, England', female)

Others spoke about racism in the city outside school:

because teenagers and people who go to football are becoming more rasist.
('I come from the Midlands', male)

racism is big in Peterborough.
('I'm white and come from uk', male)

because the brown people hit the white people.
('I'm white', female)

Four people clarified that some people were still racist despite 'You, Me and Us'. One felt that racism persisted despite 'You, Me and Us':

because some people are still being racist regardless to what we learnt.
('I am English and I'm white', male)

Another took the more positive view that 'You, Me and Us' might make things better:

because some people are still racist and if you-me-us come to our school different people would mix together and the racism might stop.
('I'm white and I'm English & me & my families from England C of E', female)

One person felt that one visit a year from 'You, Me and Us' was not enough to make an impact:

> because in 1 years is not enough.
> ('White, Christian, C of E', male)

One young person said more programmes like 'You, Me and Us' were needed because the school was not doing enough itself about racial abuse:

> because the teachers are not very strict on racism.
> ('I'm white, Christian and I come from England', female)

Summary

Many of the prejudices and opinions expressed by young people about people from different backgrounds were similar to those expressed in Stafford. Negative or intolerant attitudes, however, seemed more prevalent in Peterborough, most markedly at schools with multiracial pupil groups. So proximity to diversity seems to have made some young people less rather than more tolerant. However, those young people who attended schools with relatively large proportions of Muslim pupils seemed to have a better knowledge of the specific cultural differences between groups in the local community. So, while proximity may not have induced tolerance, it does seem to have led to a little more knowledge. Something similar emerges from the Rochdale case study in Chapter 5, where, for example, some young white people had learnt insults and slang in Punjabi from their Pakistani friends at school.

Although most young people had enjoyed the 'You, Me and Us' programme, many felt it had made little impact because they were not racist anyway. Nevertheless, a number reported that they had changed their behaviour for the better towards young people from other backgrounds. Some also said that they were, as a result of attending the programme, more likely to stand up for others experiencing racism and bullying. This last finding is different from Stafford and a significant extra achievement of this programme. The structured nature of the programme with clearly defined objectives and a range of activities and presenters are some of the factors that have contributed to the success of the programme in a community where many local practitioners feel that racial tension needs to be reduced.

3 Diversity Awareness Programme, London

Context

Since racially aggravated offences were created in the Crime and Disorder Act 1998, an increasing number of offenders have received sentences for crimes that refer specifically to the racial motive. According to the Crown Prosecution Service, between April 2002 and March 2003, 4,029 racially aggravated offences were prosecuted, of which 84 per cent were convicted. Thirteen per cent of prosecutions were for racially aggravated assaults, such as the cases discussed below. Forty-four per cent received fines, 67 per cent received community sentences and 8 per cent received custodial sentences. Just under 11 per cent (442 out of 4,029 prosecutions for racially aggravated offences) were pursued in the London Metropolitan and City Crown Prosecution Service area. The Probation Service has responsibility for addressing underlying causes of offending and to reduce the risk of reoffending. The Probation Service in London has developed programmes of one-to-one work with convicted racially motivated offenders. Merseyside is among other areas of the Probation Service that have developed similar programmes for work with racially motivated offenders.

Diversity Awareness Programme

London Probation Service practitioners and the London Probation research department, have developed an in-depth one-to-one programme for working with racially motivated and racist offenders. The aims are to reduce the risks of potential harm caused by racially motivated offending and racist attitudes, and of reoffending. The specific objectives are to confront the offender with the effect of their attitudes and behaviour on victims and also the impact on the wider community; to show offenders how and why their beliefs were formed and how this contributes to offending behaviour; to challenge offending attitudes and to develop new behaviours and attitudes; to enable offenders to develop a secure sense of their own identity; and to reiterate that racist behaviour is criminal and that persistence in these views puts offenders at risk of further offending and the public at risk. The Diversity Awareness Programme draws on other probation offender programmes, most notably anger management and thinking skills programmes. It also uses theories that inform work with other targeted offending like domestic violence and sex offending.

The programme is for offenders who have either committed a racially aggravated offence or whose behaviour indicates that they have entrenched racist attitudes, as well as behaviour that may have implications for their offending. Offenders of all ages participate in the programme. The programme has been piloted across a number of London boroughs and in one young offenders institution. At the end of 2003, over 30 offenders had undertaken the programme, the two mentioned in this research were worked with the most consistently in a young offenders institution.

The programme is facilitated and delivered by a probation officer (trained by the programme's developers) in around 20 one-to-one, one-hour sessions with the offender over at least ten weeks. The first module explores the offender's childhood and family experiences and their history of offending, to encourage the offender to reflect on the influences on their views that have contributed to their offending behaviour. It also explores the offender's family's origins and begins to explore their own sense of identity. The second module explores the offender's sense of identity in more depth and discusses the fixedness and fluidity of identity in general, and definitions of Britishness and Englishness. This module also explores the ways in which the offender 'allows himself to offend' and their motivation to change themselves. The third module covers thinking skills and how different ways of thinking impact on racist attitudes. The fourth attempts to develop victim empathy and break down the offender's denial and minimising of the seriousness of the offending behaviour and its consequences. It also seeks to clarify the difference between fact and opinion, and develop a questioning attitude towards information received from the media and family and friends. The fifth encourages the offender to think about their own experiences of being a victim to encourage victim empathy. It also encourages them to think about how they choose their victim. The sixth module attempts to make the offender aware of whether they employ unconscious racist stereotypes whenever they become angry or resentful. It also attempts to challenge negative myths associated with minority communities. The final module encourages the offender to consider the advantages of non-offending and the consequences of further offending. It also attempts to develop more positive images of black and Asian people, and to encourage the offender to think about influences that might put them under pressure to offend. In particular, it looks at strategies that will help the offender resist peer pressure.

By comparison with the programmes in Peterborough and Stafford, this programme is far more intensive, in depth, sustained over a longer period of time and, most important of all, designed to address serious racist behaviour in people with hardened beliefs and a history of aggression. The programme is the subject of ongoing evaluation.

Research approach

Joint interviews with two participants in the pilot programme at the young offenders institution were conducted with researchers at the Probation Service in December 2003. The discussions explored the young persons' experiences of being on probation and their views about the programme. In the sections below false names are used for the two young offenders to protect their anonymity.

'Bobby'

Bobby had a previous conviction for racially aggravated assault:

I had a fight with some Asian people in a shop.

Prior to his participation in the programme, he felt all Asian people stuck together and were powerful or aggressive (reflecting to some degree views expressed by some of the schoolchildren in Stafford and Peterborough). The programme had helped him comprehend that his understanding was neither full nor accurate:

I used to think that Indian people and Asian people ... stick together and that they are powerful people and things like that. I learned that ... it's just the way they are. And because of what they have been through in the past – that makes them more closer ... That makes me feel different now – if I got caught in a situation like that again, I'd realise what is happening.

The programme had also helped him to realise that people of different backgrounds were equal, something that he didn't believe before:

What I have got from this – I realise that people are equal basically.

That he was considered a racist had not occurred to him before:

I didn't know I was like that until I started talking to her [the probation officer] and then we spoke about a few things and I realised that I was what they called racist ... I didn't feel too good.

When asked if he felt he was still racist, he said:

No, I don't think I am now, no I don't think I am now.

He had volunteered to participate in the programme because he wanted to learn more about himself:

I wanted to learn about myself, basically what sort of a person I am ... Like there's things that I learned in there I didn't know before about myself ... so it's done well for me.

When asked what he had learnt, he said:

There are a lot of things that I know I need to sort out – to make sure that I don't come back to jail – things like family issues, drugs, alcohol, a lot of things. But it doesn't just cover that one thing, it covers a lot of things, from when you were young all the way until ... it was good.

The programme had helped him control his anger and resolve problems by talking rather than by the use of violence:

Every time I went to the programme, it was like a release for me, 'cause I am an angry person – when I went to these courses, these sessions, they have taken that away from me so I can talk about things, and let things out, and then you feel better ... I learned a lot about ways to deal with problems apart from with violence ... Rather than shouting and slapping people, I learned how to talk to people, things like that, instead of just going straight in and being stupid.

He was then asked how he had changed his behaviour. He replied.

Altogether, violence and the way I act towards people, the way I talk to people. I think I come across friendlier these days here on the wing, a bit more easier to talk to.

Participation in the programme would help him avoid violent confrontations in the future:

I have been in confrontations obviously, but I just deal with it differently, I just think about things that happened in the programme and I remember things to do, what to say.

He also felt that the programme had reduced the chances of him reoffending, though he still felt uncertain:

I don't think ... if I'm honest I can't say that I will not come back here, that I won't commit another crime 'cause I don't know – but I doubt that I will come back to jail for a violent offence, but I can't say never.

Bobby felt that the programme's success for him was because of the skill and dedication of the programme leader:

[The programme leader's] good, I know that, I worked well with her – it's the main thing, it's the person doing it.

He also acknowledged the strength of the material:

The programme itself is good, I think the programme will work, if they do a lot more – they should use it a lot more – they need to use a lot more things like that sort of scheme.

There was nothing about the programme he disliked and he felt nothing was missing from the programme. In his view, it worked much better on a one-to-one basis than it would in a group:

I think it would be better one-to-one. I don't think ... the thing about a group, I don't think people are honest – they're trying to act smart themselves because of other people in the room, and don't like to admit what they done. And then if you are not honest, the course ain't going to work ... One-to-one's a lot better, a lot better – people are a lot more honest.

'Tom'

Tom had been involved in an incident in an Indian restaurant:

I didn't actually do anything when it actually happened – it was my co-defendant, he just kicked off in a curry house, starts fighting and that, and I couldn't just stand there and watch so I went and helped him basically – and I only hit one person 'cause he went at me with a knife so I went and hit him and we went after that … it weren't no peer pressure, it was more a loyalty kind of thing – in that situation he would have helped me, I would guarantee 100 per cent he would have helped me, and 'cause I could see them pushing him about and that, I weren't angry or nothing at first, but I started to get angry when he pulled the knife out, that's when I got angry, 'cause they rushed me in the actual shop from behind the door, and there was eight of them just kneeing me, and my mate kicked the door open and dragged me out.

He had committed other racially motivated violent attacks:

I beat up my next-door neighbour, I don't think they're Indian, I think they're something else, but they look Indian, but they're not, they are like Mauritians or something like that.

Tom knew he was racist before he participated in the programme:

I asked for a job down on reception, I think that's how it started, yeah, and they said 'you have to do a course first' because they said I was racist and that, and so I was, although I wasn't as bad as people were making me out to be, but I admit I was.

He used to think all Asians were arrogant and had little respect for him. These views were based on his interpretation of those he had known in the past:

I used to think that all Indians are the same basically, 'cause I've always thought they were arrogant, they try and look at you like you're a piece of crap really, and I didn't like it and I used to basically think they were all the same, 'cause the ones I've had contact with, the ones I've had fights with and what have you, that's what's happened, that's what they've been like.

Tom illustrated his dislike for Asian people again when talking about the conversations he had been involved in at the young offenders institution. Knowing his views about other racial groups made it easy for others to goad him:

There were loads of complaints and stuff like that about me being racist and that, people would get into a conversation about it when I'm there and I think they deliberately do it to get me into trouble, they start conversations about Indians peoples and stuff like that, and then someone says 'so what's wrong with them?' to me, so, me being me, I didn't think and I say the first thing that comes into my head, that's what I say, so I was stitched up for that.

Tom drew attention to the influence of his immediate family on his negative attitudes towards Asian people:

My dad's the same and my brothers, they don't like 'em either, because they all think they're arrogant and all that, and I suppose they've just taught me that as well, and I've looked up and thought 'I'll think that way as well'.

Tom drew a clear distinction between Asian people and black people. He believed all black people were thieves. Nevertheless he could get on with them. Asians, on the other hand, had no respect for him:

I get on … what I've always said … I talk to black people, I get on well with them all right, but I never trust them … I don't trust them, they can be your best mate but they'll shit on you and steal from you and that's a guaranteed thing, they'll always steal from you. But Asians, you can't talk to them 'cause they'll talk down to you and I don't like being talked down to by people.

Tom felt the programme had helped him to recognise that not all Asians are the same and not to prejudge them:

I still think the people I have fights with, I still think they're probably arrogant or whatever, but I will look at other people and I won't judge them from the people that I had fights with before, but I will take the chance to like, the first impression or that kind of thing.

This change in attitude was partly brought about by recognising that, for most of his life, he had a positive relationship with one Asian family:

I've got a friend, like, well he's my brother's friend, he's an Indian bloke as well, and he's got two children and he lives about five minutes from the pub and I see him in the pub all the time and he's like an elder brother to me as well, it's like, if I've got no money then he'll give me the money, and I've been round his house for dinner and that so, but I don't really eat Indian food and that, it's not for the fact I don't like Indians, it's that I don't like spicy food kind of thing … but he made me some sort of mince chapatti thing, his wife's special thing, it was bloody lovely, he went 'go on, take this home with you', and I was eating it on the way back, and I was thinking 'shall I go back and get another one?' It was lovely … I've cut his back garden and I play with his, like his little children – he's got a little girl that, I don't really know her name, I've always known her as princess, so I have got some friends who are like Indian and that … they are people I've known since I was little, since I was three or four years old, but the people now that I first meet I do find arrogant, some of them.

Learning that people were all different and could not be seen and treated as a homogeneous and indistinguishable group had been the hardest part of the programme for him:

The hardest part was looking at the fact that they are all different … that was the hardest part because I've always believed that they are all the same … so putting it in a different perspective is harder than what I actually thought.

As well as coming to see things differently, he had also learned to better control his anger:

The way she's explained it to me, it's made me look at it all in a different way so, and it's like she's been helping me, and she's been doing a bit of anger management – it's not in the course or nothing.

He felt anger management would be a useful addition to the programme.

Me I just kick off, I mean the big things I can handle, yeah, it's the little things that annoy you, like your brother comes in and takes one of your fags out your box and he takes them without asking – that will bug me for days on end – if he took the whole box it wouldn't bug me so much. But we was working on it, she was helping me on how it all leads up like – the argument will start with a member of me family or my girlfriend, or – because I've never hit a girl, I don't hit girls or me brother or that, I go out and start drinking and where it'd pray on my mind I'd get angry, and the first person that says anything to me, I'd go whack, and that'd be it – so she's helping me realise how it all starts off and that.

He expanded on this theme again later in the conversation:

I've never actually done an anger management course, I think that's why [the programme leader] put it in as an extra bit of work kind of thing, and it helps me to realise how it's all started and that … 'cause I've never looked at things like that, but when she comes out with it, it makes it sound a lot clearer, 'cause when I try to say things like that I confuse myself and that.

Tom felt that the best part of the programme for him had been understanding how his misperception of a situation leads to anger and then to violent confrontation:

I think the best bit was, as I said earlier, when she made me look at it all in a different way by the way she was explaining it to me and the way it all leads to the actual fight – I think that was the best part.

He also felt he had learned some important things about himself – that he was a difficult and selfish person:

I realise how much of a pain in the arse I've been … I was a selfish person, I never thought about what anyone else wanted, it was all about what I wanted, and if I didn't have it I'd break something, round my mum's house I'd smash the door in or something like that. It weren't drinking, it were if I'd got a problem I'd get angry over a stupid argument, you know, like I told you about the little things that wind me up, I'd go for a drink, I'd wind myself up in the head … I'd be drinking and when I'm getting more and more drunk and that, I'd be thinking about that little thing, and I'd think worse and worse about it, and I'd make the situation a lot worse than what it is, and I'd just make things worse for myself, so, that's the main thing that I was, a selfish person.

Although he may have learnt not to stereotype Asian people, his views about black people had not changed as a result of the programme:

I don't trust them [black people], no … 'Cause they're thieves, they're thieves … my friends have had experiences like that, my cousins, all my family, my aunties, uncles and stuff like that have had their houses robbed by black people … but anyway the people that I would associate with that are black I know full well are thieves to start off with, so they never come near my house. No … you're either a thief or you're not – people can't change, it's in their blood, you're born that way.

Tom was uncertain whether the programme would lessen the chances of him reoffending:

I couldn't actually say that or not. I couldn't actually say that I plan things ahead, I just take each day as it comes. I suppose I'd look at it in a different way, I wouldn't bite straightaway where normally I would before – before, if anyone said something, I'd probably just go for them, I wouldn't even think about it, I'd just swing my fist at them, where probably now I'd just look at 'em and laugh, depending on what they're actually saying like – if they just say to me 'you're a prick' or something like that, then I'd most probably just walk away, but if they said something about my mother or called me a white bastard, I'd most probably break their hair off or something.

Tom thought the positive impact of the programme on him was largely the result of the effort that the programme leader had made to assist him with the specifics of the programme, as well as helping him more generally:

Yeah – the way it was written down, the way the questions were written down, I can't understand most of the questions, so she'll help me by explaining it in a different sort of way so I'll understand it, so it'd make it a lot easier, and it did help, and I'd start to think about things as well – she'd come in and say 'did you think about the things we did last week?' and I'd go 'yeah' – she was probably thinking to herself 'he's such a lying little git' … but I did, I thought about it quite a lot, I thought 'well she's putting in a lot of effort to help me' so I thought it's only right to make the effort back to try and think about stuff and to try and get myself back together and that.

He also valued the way the programme leader had listened to him without making judgements and treated him with respect. He said that, before these discussions with the programme leader, no one had ever really listened to his version of the events for which he was convicted:

No one ever listens to it … my solicitor, when I told him, he went up to court and gave a completely different bloody thing to what I said, so he obviously didn't listen to anything I said.

Tom was sure that the programme would not work in a group rather than one-to-one:

I'd feel uncomfortable in a group, 'cause fair enough they'd most probably tell me their problems, but I feel insecure or things like that. I don't like being in a group when I tell people how it is and that, so I'd prefer it one-to-one, it makes it easier on yourself as well. When you're in a group, it's like there's a lot of pressure on you 'cause everyone's staring at you and stuff like that, but when you're by yourself you haven't got to worry what everyone else thinks, so it's a lot easier … I would have refused to do it if it *was in a group, when I'm in a group I just muck about anyway, that's what I've always been like, it's like at school I've always been the class clown kind of thing.*

Summary

The Diversity Awareness Programme evidently corrected some stereotypes and misconceptions, increased self-awareness, including empathy with the experiences of others, and helped participants to see themselves as others see them, as well as influencing future behaviour. For all these reasons, the programme should be regarded as a well-received and successful intervention, at least in its immediate impact on the individuals. The impact on future offending remains to be seen. A sustained, in-depth, one-to-one programme that encourages reflection on experience and strengthens a positive sense of identity, challenges myths, encourages a questioning attitude towards sources of information and helps people to manage angry and violent behaviour can evidently mitigate racist behaviour. However, a programme such as this may have less impact on extreme racists with entrenched and unapologetic views.

4 Tower Hamlets Summer University, East London

Local context

Despite the revival of the Docklands and the building of Canary Wharf, Tower Hamlets in the East End of London (where most of the young people who participated in this case study live) is still characterised by high proportions of social housing, poverty and the largest concentration of Bangladeshi people anywhere in the UK. Indeed the majority of the UK Bangladeshi population live in Tower Hamlets. The heart of the Bangladeshi community is in the west of the borough, centred on Brick Lane and Bethnal Green. Many social housing estates in this area have a majority of Bangladeshi residents. In the east of the borough, around the old docks, there is still an ageing white community with few young children. Recently, new migrant communities have come to the area, including Somali families and many refugees and asylum seekers from central Africa, the Middle East and elsewhere. The combination of an older white community with few young children, large Bangladeshi families and new migrant communities with a young age profile means that young people meeting together are a highly diverse group with Bangladeshi young people often in a majority, or alternatively in exclusively Bangladeshi groups – in either case there are few white young people around.

Tower Hamlets Summer University, 'Street Life' workshops

The Summer University was first organised in 1995 in Tower Hamlets to offer constructive and free learning activities to young people during the school summer holidays. By 2003, about 10 per cent of the young people of the London Borough of Tower Hamlets attended the Summer University's activities. Activities held during the school summer holidays include classes on a wide range of subjects from Chinese brush painting to 'DJing'. The Summer University organises a volunteer programme that trains and involves young people as peer motivators and to assist in the activities throughout the summer programme.

In 2003, as part of the summer programme, a week of workshops covering social issues, collectively named 'Street Life', was piloted. A session exploring race and racism was led by Tolerance in Diversity – a group that trains young people to deliver workshops for other young people. According to the organisers, these workshops explore attitudes to and experiences of diversity, prejudice, cultural myth and division. The workshops seek to promote mediation, conciliation and reconciliation of disputes, and the understanding of the nature and causes of disputes and how to bring about peaceful resolution.

Research approach

A participatory approach was developed. Young people were involved in designing interview questions and were trained in interviewing. They then interviewed each other. With the help of the peer motivator co-ordinator, researchers organised two all-day training workshops on research skills during the half-term week of October 2003. Ten participants who were involved in the Summer University's activities in 2003 took part. Seven of the ten had been volunteer peer motivators. Of the ten young people who participated in the research, half were boys and half were girls. Their ages ranged from 12 to 20 years of age. Seven had been peer motivators. All were from black or minority ethnic communities and they lived in different neighbourhoods in East London, all of which had several different communities living in them.

The workshops offered training in research methods including different methodologies; how to structure interviews; open, closed, probing and leading questions; sensitivity and confidentiality; and recording information accurately.

The objectives of the research were outlined and the young people worked in small groups to devise questions for a structured interview. They then used the agreed version to interview each other, exploring their views about the challenges they faced; the area they lived in; relationships between local communities; their understandings and experiences of racism and identity; and their views of the Summer University scheme, the workshop on anti-racism and the experience of being a peer motivator. Once the interviews had been completed a group discussion took place. As an incentive to take part, the young people received a £10 HMV voucher and a certificate of participation in a training course on research methods.

Young people's opinions

What is racism and how big an issue is it?

The young people generally understood racism to be about disliking or abusing people, either verbally or physically, because they had a different skin colour, belonged to a different ethnic group or practised a different religion. Definitions given included:

Disliking of a whole group of people without meeting everyone of them.
(British/'Myself, everything in my own way/18')

When a person dislikes another. Reason due to their race/religion.
(British/'Me – muslim Bengali/15')

One definition focused on a lack of understanding:

someone who doesn't understand, or hasn't taken time to understand some eles. No respect for other persons belifes, cultural background.
(British/'Somalian – British/20')

Another young person focused on attitudes and beliefs. This young person was 12, the same age as many of those who completed the questionnaires in Peterborough and Stafford. She made the link between prejudice being the thought and discrimination being treating people unfairly, saying that racism was:

the way people think or treat each other from different ethnic groups.
(British/'person who is open minded/12')

Another commented:

people who believe stereotypical views of other groups and act upon them.
(British/'Muslims women/17')

Others spoke more explicitly about abusive or aggressive behaviour:

Abuse which can be physical verbal and social because of your background, realigion.
(Congolese/'Human, Black African, Christian/16')

Swearing words (verbal), Fight (physical), different skin colour, ethnic groups, feel sad.
(Bangladeshi/'Bangladeshi, Muslim/14')

I would describe (like) racism like, verbal, physical, emotional er social abuse – swearing, violence, graphics, no equality.
(British/'Hindu Bengali culture/18')

Racism was mentioned by five of the young people as among the biggest issues facing young people, but it was only one of many serious concerns including finance, low self-esteem, peer pressure, education, vandalism, drugs and alcohol, crime, bullying, anti-social behaviour, homelessness, affording university fees, sexual health and teenage pregnancy, and family troubles including divorce. When asked to describe the neighbourhoods they lived in, five of the young people described their areas in positive terms, drawing attention to peacefulness, cleanliness, security, activities, facilities and places to visit and an involved and friendly community. No one mentioned concerns such as racism or tensions between groups from different ethnic backgrounds.

This theme was expanded on in the subsequent group discussion – many participants agreed that racism was not the most pressing problem they faced. Some from a Bangladeshi background clarified that this was particularly the case in areas where they lived and spent most of their time – racism became more of a problem if they went to other areas where people with a Bangladeshi background were not perceived to be the majority. One participant from a Bangladeshi background commented:

> It depends on the area – if you went to a different area that was dominated … [where] either white or black people were the majority … and someone from the dominant group was rude to you, you would see it as racism, but if someone was rude to you in your own area and they were a member of the same group, you would just think they had a bad attitude.

When asked in their interviews whether there were tensions between different groups, six people did not think so, while four people thought there were:

> There could be some tensions – physical (fighting between different races), verbal (swearing), almost young kids, teenagers (racists).

The others suggested that tensions arose over small incidents – one young person said there was 'gang violence about stupid stuff' and another commented 'sometimes a fight occurs just for a simple reason'. The third said, 'different groups don't get along and a fight can start over girls and over little dirty looks'. Tensions sometimes arose within individual communities and not just between them. This young person thought that the differences between the Bangladeshi and western way of life could be a source of disagreement:

> Physical against same group. Bengali against Bengali. Black against Black. I see tension between Bengali culture and western culture, there way of life.

Four people said that they had experienced racism in their local community and seven said they knew other people who had suffered racism. One young man with a Hindu Bengali background had experienced verbal abuse:

> like white person asking me to go back to my country 'why don't you go there?'

One person spoke of verbal abuse that others had suffered:

> Verbal comments about the food they eat and the way they speak.

Another spoke of the impact of racist graffiti:

> Friends – everyone I know has experienced racism. Physical – verbal – writing on walls.

In the views of the participants, racism was not always perpetrated by white people. One young man with a black African background said an Asian friend's behaviour had upset him:

> A friend of mine at school, he was Asian, he drew on my hand with a black crayon and said 'I did that 'cause that's what colour you are' … I felt very hurt that my friend had done this.

One Bangladeshi girl commented:

> I saw a group of blacks boys chasing one Asian boy.

The same girl said she knew her brother had attacked a white person:

> My brother beat up a white man because he was drunk.

The experience of one family suggests that the level of racism suffered in a particular neighbourhood can vary over time. Two sisters said they had not experienced significant racial abuse, but spoke about the experiences their father had told them about, which happened a long time ago:

My father told me in 20 years, white people were beating, attacking them after the football games.

My dad, when he was younger, got ganged up on by a group of people (long time ago).

The older sister expanded on these experiences in the group discussion:

I haven't really suffered from racism, but my dad has – he was beaten up by a gang of white men about 20 years ago – he didn't want to go to hospital so a friend had to sew his head up.

Causes of racism

The responses suggested many influences on young people's racist attitudes and behaviour, including previous personal experience, perhaps leading to generalised prejudices; influence of parents and family members; belief that certain groups think they are superior; lack of understanding of other cultures; lack of tolerance of other cultures; fear of other groups through lack of understanding; historical events and peer pressure. Set out below are some of the reasons given by the respondents for the existence and persistence of racism:

family, peer pressure, ourselves – personal experience.

Family, culture (culture of there group and your own group), religion, experiences, history.

Parents can contribute like when they don't like other people from different backgrounds. Brothers and sisters – the brother may protect their sisters against other people. History: some people still hate Germany.

Racism is caused by peer pressure but not always. It sometimes comes from their family.

spreads through friends.

A strong sense of their own identity and a clear grasp of which groups lived close to them
One person described himself as both Somalian and British. Three people described themselves as Bengali and two others described themselves as British Muslims. Only one person mentioned his skin colour, describing himself as 'Human, Black, African, Christian'. One person mentioned her gender.

The young people were asked at the beginning of their interviews to describe their nationality and subsequently to describe their identity. They drew attention to the importance of their religion in the construction of their identity, along with the culture and/or place of origin of their parents or family and their own place of birth. The strength of these self-definitions did not seem to vary with age or gender in this group. Religion seemed to be a key factor – seven young people mentioned their religion: Islam for five young people, Hinduism for one and Christianity for another. One young man who described himself as 'Bangladeshi Muslim' commented:

My religion is very important along with where I come from because my parents hold these cultural traits.

For another, place of family origin was set alongside religion as the most important thing. Describing herself as 'Muslim Bengali', this young woman went on to say:

My religion is Islam, my family and I are Bangladeshi.

For another, it was religion and country of birth. A young woman aged 16 who described herself as Muslim British gave as her reasoning:

Because Islam is [my] religion and [I] was born in Britain.

In the group discussion, several people agreed with a comment that 'religion matters more than race' when thinking about their identity. Their country of origin, or that of their parents, as well as living in the UK was also important. Some participants discussed the complexities of the idea of home. One young person felt her mixed racial and cultural background allowed her to 'choose what you want to be'. Her father was Bengali and her mother was Filipino. She said she had not felt Filipino during the three years she had lived in the Philippines. Similarly she did not feel Bengali when mixing with the Bengali community in England. She, along with her sister and her mother, all thought of Britain as home, whereas their father still considered home to be Bangladesh. Some young people discussed the distinction between their Bangladeshi identity and Bangladesh the country, particularly pointing to their practical discomfort when visiting Bangladesh:

> You go there, they treat you like a princess, they think you're rich because you're from London, but I don't like it there because it's dirty.

> I could never live there because they don't have proper toilets.

While these two young women felt more at home in London than Bangladesh, despite identifying themselves as Bangladeshi, one young man was less sure whether he felt at home anywhere:

> We don't belong anywhere, it's just a place where you're born.

Another person responded however:

> I do feel I belong here ... home is where I am – you adapt to where you are, you get used to it.

The group were asked whether they were encouraged to think of their parents' country of origin as 'home'. Some young people responded that, while their parents encouraged them to think of Bangladesh as home, they did not feel this as strongly as their parents, although they still felt they had a strong link with the country.

As well as their strong sense of their own identity, they also had a strong grasp of who else lived around them. The more obvious and well-known communities living in the area are Bangladeshi, Somali and Pakistani. Many young people mentioned these groups. In addition, they mentioned Chinese, Filipino, African, Caribbean and Vietnamese communities. Some people mentioned the range of religions, referring to Christians and Muslims. One young man, who described himself as British with 'Hindu Bengali culture' and lived in Ilford, mentioned the range of places of worship:

> In my area there are 55% Asian like Mosques – muslims, temples – hindus, churches, synagogue, Indian, Pakistani, Bengladeshi. 45% English.

The Bangladeshi young people perceived themselves to be in the majority. This appeared to strengthen their own sense of identity as well as reduce the likelihood of them being the target of racist behaviour.

Some may see segregation by choice as undesirable and a barrier to community cohesion. Others, including some of the young people who attend Tower Hamlets Summer University, seem to feel that strength in numbers can mean that identity is strengthened and safety increased.

The biggest challenges of racism for this group of young people seemed to be ameliorating the influence and behaviour of peers and family members. Although these young people expressed a strong sense of identity and self-confidence, at least within their own group and local context, they seemed less certain about how they might approach unfamiliar groups of people and situations. So among the priorities for challenging and changing racist attitudes and behaviour are to strengthen their ability to challenge others, and to be as self-confident in communicating and forming relationships out of their own group and context as they are in it.

Impact of anti-racism workshop

The anti-racism workshop had an impact on a minority, but limited impact on others

Eight of the ten participants said they were not racist in the first place so the workshop had little impact on them:

I've [never] treated anyone badly due to their race.

I was good before.

I've always understood how to treat people right. I've never treated anyone badly for no reason.

However, two of the ten people felt that others might now behave better:

they are aware of what is going around them, and they don't take things for granted.

they've taught the consequences of treating people badly and have been put in the shoes of people being treated badly.

Several young people felt they now had a better understanding of the subtleties and complexities of racism and cultural differences, or that previous understandings had been reinforced. A number of people said they now had a better understanding of equality:

We are one human race.

To be equal.

Several people said they had learnt more about concepts – two people had learnt more about racism and discrimination and four others had learnt the difference between racism and prejudice. Eight learnt about 'inference ladder theory', a concept discussed at the workshop, which postulates that one negative experience with an individual of a particular racial or ethnic group influences subsequent opinions and interactions with members of the same racial or ethnic group. A number of people also said they had learnt not to prejudge people or discriminate. In response to the question 'what did you learn?', young people commented:

If you don't know a person, don't prejudice.

People can judge easily.

Treat everyone fair and be kind.

Comments in the group discussion suggested that the anti-racism workshop had been rather general; it had not been specific enough or demonstrated how the material was relevant to the participants. One person commented:

Most of the stuff I knew already. Everything was basic.

Another said it had been boring – there was 'too much talk'. Another person said:

It was boring, sorry to say. There was only sits and chats.

Some felt it would have been more effective if it had been more sustained:

I enjoyed it but I don't think it would have changed people's attitudes – it was too short and there was too much information.

The participants were asked whether projects to tackle racism were needed at all and, if so, how they might be improved. Eight people thought that more projects working with young people about the way they related to other communities were needed. Some offered the following comments:

Some people do not realise that they can be racist even through racist jokes that may be funny to one person but not to the other.

Because more information is always good and useful.

One person suggested that such programmes might help counter the influence of parents:

Parents think differently, it may influence kids.

Two people felt that more programmes were not needed. One suggested young people were taught how to behave properly anyway:

People has been brought up to know what is right and wrong.

Some young people suggested possible improvements. A number of these involved using more lively and interactive methods:

Make it more lively (music).

Have more outside activities.

Taking us to relevant trips (educational).

It shouldn't be completely different but they should use what teens enjoy e.g. music, art, going to cinema, to show curtain idea.

Some felt a more hands-on approach, which allowed them to learn by participation, would be more effective:

More hands on stuff, more activities, more places to visit.

More active. Getting people with more experience beforehand (had first hand experienced). Learn more actively (hands on experience yourself).

Another person added that its approach needed to be more rooted in real-life experiences:

More real life situation.

The young people were specifically asked whether the anti-racism workshop had helped them think more about their identity. Three said yes and seven said no. Of those that said yes, comments included:

Made me realise what things are important to me – nationality, religion.
(British Muslim)

This young person noted that the perceptions of others of your identity might be more important than your own opinion:

Made me think am more myself. Made me think about my own identity and people asking me about my ethnic origin, I get bored and I realize it doesn't matter at all to me, but it matters to everyone else.
(Islamic Bangladeshi father and Catholic Filipino mother)

Those who said that the anti-racism workshop had not helped them to think more about their own identity commented:

Because I still am a Bengali Muslim + it didn't make me change my mind.

Because I still think I am British and a Muslim.

They were also asked whether they felt young people needed more help to think about their identity: three said yes and six said no. One of the people who said yes said this was because:

People don't think about who they are and what their identity is.

However, those who said no did not see much point in exploring this. One suggested identity was obvious:

I'm sure people know who they are.

Another said race and religion were fixed and defining factors:

Because they'll always describe their identity related to their religion or/and their race.

One of the others thought identity was more a matter of choice:

They pick their identity as they grow and they stick to it, it's for them to choose their identity.

Building relationships

One of the aims of the Summer University is to build relationships, respect and mutual trust between young people from different backgrounds. However, the young person with a Bengali Hindu background felt progress on this was limited because virtually all those who attended the Summer University were from the same cultural background – Bangladeshi Muslim:

First of all, in the Summer Uni there were all one groups of people from the same culture, background as the majority.

He suggested:

Change programmes, make different people to come and join, like white or black people.

The organisers of the Summer University conceded this point. The peer motivators' co-ordinator commented:

The majority of the young people in the Summer University are Bangladeshis. We find it much harder to attract white, Somali and Chinese young people … This year we didn't do any targeting in the recruitment of the volunteers, but we didn't get a very balanced result – almost everyone was from a Bangladeshi background. Next year we intend to target the recruitment of volunteers to get broader representation.

Summary

The relatively negative observations made about the anti-racism workshop suggest that the focus was not quite right. The issue for many Bangladeshi young people is not so much that they experience or perpetrate overtly racist behaviour. Instead, the lack of mixing between young people of different cultural backgrounds and intergenerational misunderstanding are perceived as greater problems. Future programmes will need to develop the skills of enquiry, listening and empathy in young people so they may begin to communicate across divisions and, by and by, build trust and friendships.

The strengths of the Stafford and Peterborough projects – that they had clear objectives, were well structured and young people participated in a range of different activities – appear to have been less evident here. Exploration through discussion seems to have been less of a hit with some young people. Although participants in the Summer University are older than the school children in Peterborough, there is still a need for activity, interactivity and variety. The strengths of the Diversity Awareness Programme (see Chapter 3) seemed to be that it was reflective, one-to-one and sustained, as well as being structured and stimulating. Again, the Summer University programme did not seem to have these qualities. The anti-racism workshop had been led by young people, but that does not seem to have led to a more positive response.

5 Jubilee Football Tournament, Rochdale

Local context

Rochdale is home to a significant minority community – 10 per cent of the people who live there identified themselves as Asian or Asian British in the 2001 census. Eight per cent said they were Pakistani and 1 per cent said they were Bangladeshi. Nine per cent said they were Muslim. The south Asian communities in Rochdale grew substantially in the late 1950s and throughout the 1960s. Many men arriving in Rochdale in the period came from the Punjab region of West Pakistan and a relatively small proportion came from the Sylhet region of then East Pakistan, now Bangladesh. In the main, they came to take up work in the textile industry, which then declined sharply in the 1980s.

As in many northern towns, Rochdale's Asian communities are concentrated in a small number of inner-city neighbourhoods, creating *de facto* residential and social segregation. Ninety-six per cent of the borough's Pakistani community live in the five inner-city wards that are among the most deprived wards in the North West. Despite dissatisfaction with the old Victorian, privately owned, overcrowded terraced houses, there is still a strong loyalty and affection for these areas, particularly because of strong family and community ties, and proximity to mosques and shops. There is also a widespread fear that moving to other areas will increase the likelihood of racial harassment.

For the purposes of this case study, the area of Rochdale in which the football tournament took place has been given a fictitious name: 'Newton'. It is a small estate of modern, low-rise street housing owned by a large national housing association. Most of the people living in these properties are white, many of Irish descent. This small estate backs onto the area called here 'Fern Street' (again fictitiously) and other streets of small Victorian terraced houses. Most of the people who live in Fern Street are of Pakistani background, living in

owner-occupied and private rented housing. Some of the housing is owned and managed by a relatively small Asian-led housing association. The people in these two communities rarely mix and mingle socially, despite the close proximity in which they live. The distance perceived by locals is as much social as physical.

According to the community development worker employed by the large housing association, youth crime is generally high, committed by both white and Asian young people. Violent crimes have also been committed. A group of predominantly white young people are, reportedly, the main perpetrators and 'dominate' the area.

Background to the Jubilee Football Tournament

The objective of the organisers of the Jubilee Football Tournament in 2002 was to build and strengthen relationships between white young people from Newton and Asian young people from Fern Street. Despite the close proximity in which the two communities lived, familiarity and friendship were not much apparent and some tension was evident. The immediate stimulus for organising the football tournament was to improve the chances of receiving funding to develop the football pitch. Originally, two separate funding applications were planned to lay football pitches on open spaces on both the Newton estate and in the Fern Street area. The two funding applications were in effect in competition with each other. It was believed that the chances of success would be increased if the two communities worked together and made a single application.

The project was organised by a community development worker employed by the large housing association, a local authority youth worker and the residents' association for the Newton estate. The project was aimed at young people between nine and 15 years old from the two communities. Parents assisted with training and community premises owned by the large housing association were used.

Research approach

With the help of the community worker from the large housing association, a Saturday afternoon football session was arranged in March 2003. Young people from the Newton and Fern Street estates were invited to play football on the Newton estate and afterwards to participate in a group discussion. As an incentive to participate, a session at local evening football facilities for the young people who attended was booked and paid for. Ten boys and one girl between the ages of ten and 15 took part in a discussion in the Newton community house. All were white and lived on the Newton estate. The young people from Fern Street were not able to attend, apparently because they had commitments at the local mosque.

The young people who attended discussed their views on the neighbourhood and what it was like to live there; other neighbouring communities and estates; attitudes to racial and cultural difference and racism; and what the young people felt about the football tournament and the proposed pitch. After the discussion, some of the young people walked round the neighbourhood with researchers, describing points of interest.

As the Asian young people from Fern Street had not been able to attend the discussion group, their views and perspectives needed to be sought on another occasion. After some difficulties and delays, a discussion with the Asian young people who live on Fern Street took place in the local mosque in December 2003. Fifty-five young people attended a facilitated discussion with a researcher, Mosque leaders and two members of staff from the Asian-led housing association. Three boys were aged 14 and the others were 11 or 12 years of age. There were approximately 35 boys and 20 girls. This discussion focused on similar issues to those discussed with white young people: how they felt about the area where they lived; the facilities available for young people in the area, particularly sports facilities; experiences of the football tournament; friendships; experiences of racism and fights out of school.

Young people's opinions

Friends at school

Young people from both communities described how they all knew each other at school, but did not socialise much outside school. Some young white people told us, for example, about the young people they knew at school who lived in Fern Street:

Boy 1:   *Two of them are in my class.*

Boy 2:   *I used to go to school with them so I know them.*

Facilitator: *Do you have any close friends from Fern Street? Are you really good friends with anyone from Fern Street?*

Boy 7:   *Yes, this boy from my class.*

Facilitator: *But apart from playing football, do you hang out together?*

Boy 7:   *No.*

Some of the Asian boys also had white friends who lived on the other estate. Some older boys, aged around 14, said they knew people from Newton at school, but didn't hang around with them at home:

Facilitator: *Do you mix with the white lads?*

Boy 5:   *Yes.*

Facilitator: *Right, but you don't mix outside of school?*

Boy 5:   *No.*

Facilitator: *Why's that?*

Boy 5:   *Don't know.*

Some of the Asian girls who attended the discussion at the mosque also said they had white friends at school:

Some of them go to my school and are nice to me. They're nice, but some of them are bad.

Some of the young white people knew how to say insulting phrases in Punjabi, which they said they had learnt at school from young people who lived on Fern Street. One boy quoted a phrase in Punjabi meaning 'your mother is a sheep', for example. Another white young person argued he had been the victim of something like racial discrimination at the hands of his school teachers when he had shown an interest in learning Urdu:

We got this leaflet in our school saying we had to choose whether to do German, Urdu and French, and I ticked Urdu, and then when I started school they wouldn't let me do it – I had to do French. They don't want you to do Urdu, they think you might be taking the mickey out of them ... Because we're white.

Notwithstanding these positive reflections on friendships at school, one of the younger white boys suggested that relationships at school weren't quite as good as others were suggesting:

Just yesterday a gang of whites and a gang of Asians had a big fight.

Segregation outside school

By contrast to these friendships at school, young people from both communities painted pictures of distance, segregation and an absence of shared interests outside school. The white young people said that the Asian young people had a 'practice football and cricket place in the mosque', but only two of the 15 young white people said they would go there to play. According to the white young people, some young people from the Asian area had come to Newton to play football while the tournament was on. Although the two communities were organised as teams in competition with each other, some intermingling nevertheless took place after the match:

We just played their estate against ours. But we have mixed up before, after a proper match, we mix up and have a kick around.

Boys from the Asian community around Fern Street confirmed the sense of social segregation. They told researchers that, although they were keen on football, contrary to the comment above, they did not play on the pitch on the large housing association's estate. Some white young people suggested that the two communities didn't mix because they had different interests – in particular, Asian young people preferred cricket whereas the white young people preferred football:

Boy 7:   *Everyone one is football mad – crazy.*

Boy 8:   *Except for them, they like the old cricket business ... We went there and said to them 'do you want a game of soccer?'. And they said to us 'do you want a game of cricket?'. But we don't know how to play cricket.*

One of the Asian boys from Fern Street confirmed that, in his view, the white boys from Newton wouldn't play cricket with them:

They don't play with us at cricket, they don't like it, they only like football.

Tensions lead to racial harassment according to the Asian young people

Several of the young Asian people described their experiences of racism – they described verbal and physical racist abuse they had suffered at the hands of their white neighbours:

When we go [to the playing field] *they start causing fights ... when we go and play they start calling us 'Pakis' ... the white people call us names and we get racism if we go there to play football.*

Some of the Asian girls described the racist abuse they had experienced. They described being called names and in some instances violence:

Facilitator: *What do the bad ones do?*

Girl 1:   *They're racist. [We] get called names and stuff.*

Girl 2:   *Sometimes they might bang you up.*

Facilitator: *Does that mean you get beat up?*

Girl 2:   *Yes.*

Facilitator: *Has that happened to other people here?*

Children: *Yes. [Several]*

The girls clarified that both boys and girls perpetrated the racism they experienced.

The Asian boys were also sceptical about the idea of mixed teams:

Facilitator: *'Do you think it's because it's like Asians and whites playing? If it was mixed-up teams do you think it would be better?'*

Boy 15:   *They won't pass you the ball, they're selfish.*

Facilitator: *If it was six-a-side and it's three whites and three blacks in the same side – the whites won't pass you the ball?*

Boy 15:   *Yeah, and then, we have to pass the ball between ourselves. They won't pass it.*

But racism was not a problem according to white young people. The young white people also talked unprompted about racism but from entirely the opposite perspective – they stressed that they knew it was a bad thing and they weren't racist. The reason Asian people from Fern Street didn't come to play football anymore, according to the white young people, was not racism – though, confusingly, it was at least in part the result of racial differences:

The kids from Fern Street, the Muslims, they used to come up and play us but now they don't bother. They ain't got a pitch, we have a pitch here. They aren't white and they aren't British. We're not racist, we're all mates, that's the best bit about living around here.

The white young people consistently maintained they didn't dislike their Asian neighbours, although they did note a number of reasons why they wouldn't want to live in Fern Street – these reasons reflected local factors, rather than more general racial prejudices:

The roads are really busy there, and Muslims live there … and smack dealers.

One boy commented on the security arrangements that the Asian residents of Fern Street made:

They've got cages on them … 'cause they get their windows smashed.

Some of the young boys went on to complain about the smell of curry:

And it stinks down there as well – of curry.

On the other hand, the white young people did not think that the local fish and chip shop gave out any distinctive smells.

Some of the young white people's comments suggested a fear of being outnumbered by their Asian neighbours, that there were 'too many' of them, as in the following exchange:

Facilitator: *Would you take any of the kids from Fern Street onto your team? Would you like to have a mixed team?*

Boy 25:   *Yeah, but there's too many of them, there's loads of them when they're all together.*

Tensions between young people and adults

Some of the white young people made negative comments about staff at the local Asian restaurant.

While the boss at the restaurant, they said, treated them well, the other staff did not. These local concerns were linked to international themes being discussed by the media at the time: weapons of mass destruction in Iraq and the arrest of Muslims in north London for making the chemical weapon, ricin:

Facilitator: *What about from the Indian restaurant, would you go down there and get a curry?*

Boy 22: *Yes, yes, the Balti, but it's the ricin!*

Facilitator: *The ricin? What's the ricin?*

Boy 22: *A poison, anthrax, it poisons you.*

Facilitator: *The rice is poisonous?*

Boy 22: *No, ricin … 'cause there might be a big war. In London, there's ricin in the curries in Indian restaurants, so that's why we don't go down there, and those cans, they've got rats in them, rats behind the fridge.*

Facilitator: *Where did you hear about the ricin?*

Boy 23: *On the news, in London – they're making bombs!*

Facilitator: *They're making bombs – do you think so?*

Boy 23: *We've seen them making bombs in the restaurant. We went into the Balti House and they said 'get out before I break your legs'.*

Facilitator: *What, the owner?*

Boy 24: *No, not the owner, Mohammed, is on holiday in Pakistan, so the others just reckon they're the boss. They speak in their own language and they start laughing at us. But Mohammed is okay.*

The young Asian people's dislike and sense of separation from their white neighbours was evidently influenced by the racist behaviour they had been subjected to, as already described. However, their community leader perhaps reinforced their sense of apartness. He sought to protect his community from not only racism but also cultural influences that threatened the values of their community as he perceived them. He suggested that young white people behaved badly by comparison with the young Asian people because the Asian people had a strong community and good parents, where the importance of good behaviour and respecting Islamic values was stressed, whereas the white people had none of that:

They [the young white people] *have not any religious activities, they just go to school, come back, they don't have activities – these, our children, they have activities, here, in their houses, their parents they tell you 'Pray. Do not do any wrong things.'*

In his fashion, the community leader had sought to build bridges with their neighbours by holding an 'Open Mosque' day, but he was nevertheless keen that the young Asian people should be able to have their own football facilities rather than share with the young white people:

Why you bringing to the again these people, all your discussion 'go to there'? … All is not right, you calling these people 'go there', why not make round here? … People pay council tax, people pay tax, they live here, they work … You are not providing this facility to your tenants … these are your tenants!

Impact of the Jubilee Football Tournament

The young Asian people suggested young people from the two communities did spend time together and relationships may have been strengthened during the football tournament. Once the young people started to spend time with each other in a non-structured and non-supervised context, however, the young Asian people reported that they began receiving racial abuse again:

Boy 11: *We don't go in there no more, we used to play but they started fights with us a lot.*

Boy 12: *We stopped, like three months after the tournament … They started to give us trouble, we got called names, and they kick you.*

Boy 13: *They foul you.*

Boy 14: *When you go there, it's like the only people that are allowed to play football are the white people.*

The white young people felt the project had had a positive influence, strengthening friendships, although they were not specific. They also said that they were already friends before the project anyway:

Facilitator: *Do you think that when you had the competition last year you learnt more about the people from Fern Street?*

Children: *Yeah.*

Facilitator: *Do you think that playing Fern Street has brought the two estates closer together in any way?*

Children: *Yes.*

Facilitator: *Have you learnt about one another? Have you made any new friends from Fern Street?*

Children: *No, we already knew them.*

Some of the young Asian people were keen to become involved in another football tournament, but others were more wary, fearing more abuse, suggesting that perhaps the way the football project had been organised had actually made things worse, deterring some of the young Asian people from thinking about getting involved with the white people ever again:

Facilitator: *If there was another tournament, would you make a team and enter the competition?*

Children: [Some say yes, some say no.]

Facilitator: *Why not?*

Boy 26: *We'd just get racial abuse again.*

Some had come to the conclusion they would rather just have their own football facilities:

Boy 27: *Can't you make another pitch round our end?*

Facilitator: *Why would you rather have a pitch over here?*

Boy 27: *It's not fair to make us go over there.*

This young person qualified his reasons after a moment's thought, arguing that young Asian girls shouldn't be in the same company as older white boys:

Boy 27: *It's not fair to make girls go there, it's not nice for these girls to be around big lads.*

The comments of some of the Asian girls also suggest that the project focused on boys' interests, needs and relationships, ignoring those of girls. When the Asian girls were asked about football, very few were interested:

Girl 3: *Can't we have a park? It won't cost as much as a football pitch.*

Facilitator: *How should it be improved, to make it a park?*

Girl 3: *Get swings and a slide, seesaws.*

Facilitator: *Are there any girls who would like to play football?*

Girl 3: *Not me.* [Two say yes.]

Events following the football tournament

Following the tournament, a steering group to develop the joint football pitch was set up, including some young people who had participated in the football tournament. The youngest was 12 years old. Six Asian young people and four white regularly attended – again possibly evidence of growing familiarity and trust. This steering group participated in the Newton Community Development Group, which was leading applications for funding to develop the football pitch.

As a postscript, between the first discussion with young white people in Newton in March 2003 and the second with young Asian people from Fern Street in December 2003, the funding application for a football pitch in Newton got the go-ahead. The application for the football pitch in Fern Street had been rejected. The reason given for this was technical – the council was not willing to underwrite new public spaces because of the potential expense and risk associated with public liability. In Newton, however, the large housing association was able to take responsibility for the public liability associated with the pitch, which meant it could go ahead, while, because of these problems, no football pitch was to be built at Fern Street. This success for Newton removed the incentive to continue with a football project – they now had a new pitch. However, while there was to be physical investment in a new 'public space' for all the young people of the area, the comments above suggest that significant social barriers might prevent young people from the Asian community being able to benefit from this 'public space'. This remains, at the time of writing, unaddressed.

Summary

The football tournament does initially seem to have brought young people from the two communities closer together for the duration of the tournament, perhaps building on friendships and contacts that already existed at school. The extent of the mixing, however, was limited. The two neighbourhoods had separate football teams in the Jubilee Tournament. Young people from both communities expressed little enthusiasm for mixed teams, so those bridges had not been built. The football tournament did not have as its ambition the wish to challenge prejudice or combat racist abuse and behaviour – nor evidently did it succeed in doing so. In this sense, this project lacked the specific clarity of anti-racist purpose noted in Stafford (see Chapter 1), Peterborough (see Chapter 2) and the Diversity Awareness Programme (see Chapter 3). Perhaps building bridges was hard enough, though some discussion on these issues as well as playing football does not seem completely inconceivable and would certainly have been welcome in the light of comments from the young Asian people about their experiences of racism. In virtually all areas of discussion there were significant differences of perception between the white and Asian young people. That alone represents a significant problem. Inaction is regrettable.

Nevertheless, building trust and friendship is an important and serious goal in itself and the absence of this aspiration in the other more explicitly anti-racist activities already described in the other towns is, in a different way, also a matter of regret. But the most important missed opportunity in terms of the football project's stated goal of bringing communities together was that the bridge-building sports activities (and others more inclusive of girls) did not continue after the end of the football tournament. A well-established building block was regrettably not built on. The community builders appear to have rejected a building block that might have become a cornerstone.

6 Findings and implications

Findings

Young people's prejudices

The significant minority of young people who admitted to disliking members of other groups were asked which groups they disliked and why. The reasons were many and varied. Muslims and Asians, as well as Afghanis and Iraqis, were considered by some young people to be potential terrorists following the attacks on the US in September 2001, and the wars in Afghanistan and Iraq. The surrounding publicity and political debate may have had as much impact on the attitudes of young people as the events themselves. Refugees and asylum seekers are also perceived by some young people to be potentially hijackers or terrorists. Refugees and asylum seekers are thought by some to receive preferential treatment.

Perceptions persist among some young people that minority ethnic communities are not entitled to live in Britain and should be in their own country. Some young people feel that the UK will be overwhelmed by minority ethnic communities. They are also said by some not to obey the widely accepted laws and norms of British society. Some also see minority ethnic communities as the source, not the victim of hostility. Asian people are believed by some young people to look down on white people.

Some young people say they just dislike difference. Black Caribbean communities continue to be associated with crime in the minds of some young people. On the other hand, some black and minority ethnic young people believe many white people are nasty, arrogant and racist.

Sources of prejudices

Family and friends are among the most powerful influences; perhaps adults might have expressed views rather like those expressed by young people. Some young people had been on the wrong end of a bad experience with a member of another community. That experience had tainted their view of the entire group – in some instances, other communities too. Events in local communities – well-publicised racially motivated crimes, for example – can also fuel prejudice and intolerance. Beyond immediate personal, local or domestic experiences and influences, the media, particularly in its reporting of international affairs and the views of politicians about international affairs, bears a responsibility for allowing misconceptions to grow. These misconceptions can then be inaccurately applied across whole groups in society. These many sources of prejudice and hostility can intermingle, like the tributaries of a river, producing a confusing torrent of images and ideas where fact merges with fiction, television images interchange with reality, personal experience coalesces with half-understood received opinions.

Although the influences are similar, a greater proportion of boys than girls admit to intolerant attitudes. Girls seem, on the whole, also to be more aware of the intolerant attitudes of others, believing that there is more dislike and unfairness around than boys do. Nevertheless a significant proportion of girls also express prejudices.

Young people's understanding of racism

Young people who participated in the range of research methods in these five case studies think of racism as prejudiced and intolerant attitudes that can lead to unfair treatment or racially motivated abuse or aggression: racist name calling and bullying, for example. They see racism as bad thoughts and worse behaviour. Racism, in the way they define it, can be perpetrated by anyone, not just by white people. Nor do they think of skin colour as the only provocation to racist attitudes and behaviour. Religion and cultural differences can also be sources of intolerance. Religion as a signifier of intolerance appears to be growing in importance in relations between young people. Skin colour as the main way of dividing the races appears, on the other hand, to be receding. One young person noted that, for them, 'religion is more important than race'. This reflects wider changes of perception in politics and the media particularly in relation to members of Muslim communities. The attacks on the World Trade Centre and the Pentagon as well as the wars in Afghanistan and Iraq have inflicted collateral damage on relations between young people in communities in the UK with substantial Muslim populations – even though in the main the Muslim communities in the UK have their roots in countries that are not involved in international disputes. This is unsurprising, but depressing.

Young people do not, on the whole, think of racism as a system of power relations in which white people tend to hold the superior positions and people of colour hold the inferior positions; they see it as bad thoughts and worse behaviour.

Multicultural communities do not necessarily inculcate more tolerant attitudes in young people

Comparing the results from the diverse city of Peterborough with the results from the smaller and more monochrome town of Stafford, it seems that the proportion of young people with intolerant attitudes is greater in places where communities of different racial backgrounds live in close proximity. In Peterborough, as in Rochdale, proximity has not led to familiarity or friendship. Young people live segregated social lives outside school. Contacts between families are few and friendships between young people from different background when outside school are far between. Despite this, a significant minority think they know enough of each other to harbour dislike. On the other hand, in places like Stafford with few minority ethnic residents, smaller proportions of young people expressed explicit racial or religious prejudices.

Impact of activities to challenge and change the racist attitudes and behaviour of young people

What is being achieved

Many formal education initiatives undertaken as part of citizenship or PHSE education seek to impart a powerful core message: racist name calling and bullying is wrong and hurtful. This is admirable and the message seems to successfully get through. Many programmes also contain an implicit and often explicit message that all are equal. Again an admirable thought and, indeed, half of the foundation of universal human rights, the other half being freedom.

Among young people, beliefs about tolerance appear to be spread across a spectrum. Some young people seem to be very open-minded as well as being aware of the unfairness of others. Other young people have a less clear-cut positive outlook, but do not necessarily harbour deeply held prejudices that lead them to act unfairly or aggressively. At the other extreme, some young people appear to be committed to prejudices and intolerant attitudes and behaviour. Educational activities and community projects intended to combat racist attitudes and behaviour seem to have the greatest effect on the middle group. Among the projects evaluated in this research, key factors that have a positive impact on the young people's experience of the project seem to be:

- well-defined objectives, not necessarily about only anti-racism

- a clear structure

- a range of activities, presenters and facilitators

- sustained activities over time; one-off events make less impact

- encouraging reflection on personal experiences and inquiry into local circumstances

- encouraging different attitudes and behaviour in the future.

What is not being achieved

Unfortunately the messages that aggression is wrong and everyone's equal do not reach the heart of the matter. Since many young people do not in any event believe that they are guilty of racist name calling or bullying, this is reinforcing an existing belief. The message that all are equal can, if not carefully presented and handled, slide easily into the message we are all the same. Since it is evident even to very young children that we are not all the same, this message is confusing and misleading, perhaps leading young people to think that adults are hiding from the truth or, worse still, hiding the truth from them. The conclusion that may be drawn therefore is that the best way not to upset adults is to abide by their taboos, even though they are plainly wrong. Young people may not have learnt right from wrong; instead they have learnt what adults can and, more importantly, cannot cope with, which was not the idea at all.

Combating the contemporary manifestations of racist and religious prejudices and discrimination, and building the social capital between communities that would characterise community cohesion would require greater ambition. A sustained educational initiative with an outcome of reducing racism would need to follow a trajectory something like the following.

Stage 1   Prejudiced attitudes (not just bad behaviour) would have to be challenged and uprooted.

Stage 2   Insight and empathy into the identity and experience of others would have to be induced.

Stage 3   Difference would need to be understood – currently young people, among others, simply don't seem to know what to ask each other about their differences or what they would make of the answers.

Stage 4   Common ground needs to be found; shared values agreed on.

Stage 5   Friendships must grow.

Stage 6   Mutual obligations must be created.

Implications: what would help reach these higher ambitions?

Reflect on personal experience; debate local events; learn through experience

Activities that encourage young people to reflect on their own experiences and debate local events and concerns are more likely to have a lasting impact than presenting general information about racism, which seems distant and superficial and therefore of little relevance. As well as discussing personal experiences and local events, experiential learning, which has a greater capacity to surprise or to reach less rational beliefs, or beliefs that people are reluctant to admit to, is also likely to be an important component. If the intention is to seek to remove entrenched or aggressively held prejudices, one-to-one activities are more likely to work than group activities.

Strengthening everyone's sense of identity

Activities designed to explore and understand difference are not just in order to increase understanding of other people. They should also help young people to understand themselves better and thereby strengthen their own sense of identity. Talking about myself might reveal to me how little I know about myself and my own heritage and that I might benefit from finding out more, for myself as well as in order to discuss questions of identity with others. That does, of course, require young people from majority communities to give up the space marked 'normal'. Thinking of oneself as normal and everyone else as different is not a stimulus to curiosity, much less learning.

Going beyond challenging discrimination: bringing young people together to build empathy and trust over a sustained period

Challenging unfairness is an important ambition, but in changing times more is needed. Diversity, though valued by many (usually those who are well off and not threatened), has in some places led to division. Young people from divided or segregated groups that live in close proximity without much familiarity (whether the divisions are racial, religious or have some other source) need to be brought together in a structured and sustained way, perhaps by participating in discussions and activities in which they can build shared experiences and aspirations. These activities should appeal to girls as well as to boys. These need not necessarily be focused on anti-racism. Sport and arts activities, or activities to the general benefit of the neighbourhood, sustained over an extended period may well produce the deeper bonds of empathy and trust that will build durable coalitions against intolerance. Empathy and trust lead to a sense of mutual obligation. That coalition against intolerance and those mutual obligations might, in an old-fashioned way, be called friendship.

Appendix 1

Questions asked in Stafford schools

Sport

1 Write down your favourite football team in the box below or,

2 If you don't have a favourite team because you don't like football then tick the box below.

Music

3 Which ONE of the following bands/singers is YOUR favourite?

Religion/faith

4 Do you recognise any of the following religious symbols? Beside each picture write down what religion/faith you think it belongs to?

5 Where do you and your family regularly go to pray?

People, groups and communities

6 What are the main different racial communities that live in Stafford? (Try and list three groups if you can.)

7 Do you think that any of the different groups of people are DISLIKED by other groups of people in Stafford?

8 Which groups of people are most disliked and why?

9 Do YOU think that there are …
   a   … too many different people from different racial communities in England
   b   … a good mix of different people from different racial communities in England?

10 If you think there are too many different communities or groups of people in England which one(s) do you think there are too many of?

Behaviour and attitudes

11 What is prejudice?

12 What is discrimination?

13 What is racism?

14 Are there any particular racial communities or groups that you dislike?

15 If YES, what racial communities or groups do you dislike?

16 Why do you DISLIKE those groups of people?

17   Do you think it is okay to dislike or call people names because they happen to be a different colour, religion or from another country than you?

18   Why do you say that?

'Show Racism the Red Card'

19   Did you enjoy the video, *Show Racism the Red Card*, and the activities with PC [name] when she came to the school?

20   What did YOU enjoy the MOST about the video and the activities with PC [name]?

21   What did YOU dislike the MOST about the video and the activities with PC [name]?

22   What did you learn from the video and the activities with PC [name]?

23   Do you think that the video and activities with PC [name] have made you think and feel differently about people who may be a different colour or religion from you?

24   In what ways has it made you think and feel differently about people who are a different colour or religion from you?

About you

25   Are you ...? Boy / Girl

26   How old are you?

27   How would you describe YOUR racial identity?

28   How would you describe your parents' racial identity?

29   How many of your friends are from the following racial communities?

30   Where do you live in Stafford?

31   Do your parents go to work?

Appendix 2

Questions asked in Peterborough schools

First questionnaire

Sport

1   Write down your favourite football team in the box below or,

2   If you don't have a favourite team because you don't like football then tick the box below.

Music

3   Which ONE of the following bands/singers is YOUR favourite?

Religion/faith

4   Do you recognise any of the following religious symbols? Beside each picture write down what religion/faith you think it belongs to?

5   Where do you and your family regularly go to pray?

People, groups and communities

6   In YOUR view, what are the main different racial groups of people that live in Peterborough? (Try and list three groups if you can.)

7   Do YOU think that there are … 'too many different people from different racial communities in Peterborough'?

8   If you ticked Box 1 (i.e. there were too many different people from different racial communities) which racial communities do you think there are too many of in Peterborough?

9   Do you think that any of the different groups of people are DISLIKED by other groups of people in Peterborough?

10 Which groups of people are most disliked and why?

Behaviour and attitudes

11 What is prejudice?

12 What is discrimination?

13 What is racism?

14 Are there any particular racial communities or groups that you dislike?

15 If YES, what racial communities or groups do you dislike?

16 Why do you DISLIKE those groups of people?

17 Do you think it is okay to dislike or call people names because they happen to be a different colour, religion or from another country than you?

18 Why do you say that?

19 Have YOU ever been unfriendly or aggressive towards people from other racial communities or groups?

20 If YES, which racial group(s)/communities were you unfriendly towards and why?

21 Have people from other racial communities ever been unfriendly or aggressive towards YOU?

22 If YES, what did they say/do and WHY do you think they were unfriendly towards you?

About you

23 Are you ...? Boy/Girl

24 How old are you?

25 How would you describe YOUR racial identity?

26 How would you describe your parents' racial identity?

27 How many of your friends are from the following racial communities?

28 Which part of Peterborough do you live?

29 Do your parents go to work?

Second questionnaire

'You, Me and Us'

1 Did you enjoy the workshops and activities on the YOU-ME-US project when it came to the school on Monday 10th March?

2 Why do you say that?

3 What, if anything, did you learn from the different workshops and activities on that day? If you learned nothing, say why you didn't learn anything.

4 What part(s) of the YOU-ME-US project did YOU enjoy MOST? Briefly say why you liked that/those part(s) the most.

5 What part(s) of the YOU-ME-US project did YOU dislike the MOST? Briefly say why you disliked that/ those part(s)

6 Has the YOU-ME-US project made you THINK/FEEL differently about racism and people who may be a different colour, have a different religion or be from a different country than you?

7 If YES, in what ways, if any, has it made you think and feel differently? If NO, why do you say that?

8 Has the YOU-ME-US project made you BEHAVE differently towards other people who may be a different colour, have a different religion or be from a different country than you?

9 If YES, in what ways has your behaviour changed? If NO, say why not.

10 Would you like to see anything done differently on the YOU-ME-US project? If YES, say what you would change. If NO, say why you said NO.

11 Would you like to see more projects, such as YOU-ME-US, that deal with the issue of racism come to YOUR school?

12 Why do you say that?

13 Do you have anything else you would like to say about the YOU-ME-US project? (You can say whatever you want.)

About you

14 Are you ...? Boy / Girl

15 How old are you?

16 How would you describe YOUR racial identity? (*Racial identity refers to a person's skin colour, their religion, their culture and/or the country they or their parents come from.*)

17 How would you describe your parents' racial identity? (*Racial identity refers to a person's skin colour, their religion, their culture and/or the country they or their parents come from.*)

18 Which part of Peterborough do you live in?

19 Do your parents go to work?